HERE'S WHAT OTHERS ARE SAYING ABOUT RAISING MORE MONEY

The Ask Event model is a masterpiece! Our "Lighting the Way" event generated about $460,000 in gifts and pledges from 200 guests and leadership donors. Board members were ecstatic, and guests overwhelmed us with superlatives, both at the event and in our Follow-Up Calls. We're energized, re-inspired, empowered. Now that we know what's possible, there'll be no stopping us next year!
— **Kay Baumgartner, Development Associate**
  The Osborne Association, Long Island City, NY

We scrupulously followed the rules of the Raising More Money Model and received over $300,000 in 59 minutes at our first Ask Event! Thank you to Raising More Money for the model and to our coach for outstanding training and support!
— **Twink Lynch, Ph.D., Board Member**
  Topeka Civic Theatre and Academy, Topeka, KS

In a time when donors are expecting more from our development offices than an annual request, the Raising More Money Model offers us a systematic way to build donor relationships by connecting donors personally to the impact their gifts are having on the lives of others. By bringing them inside our mission, we have been able to convert prospects to donors and small donors to our strongest supporters.
— **Jeannette Archer-Simons, CEO**
  Girl Scouts, Connecticut Trails Council, Inc., North Haven, CT

Thanks to Raising More Money's training, our Ask Event was a huge success! It raised the profile of our college beyond our wildest expectations and opened doors that would never have opened for us otherwise. We've received media coverage, found new partners, and developed better connections between staff and the community. The Raising More Money strategy has assisted us in creating a more vibrant, engaging work environment.
— **Elaine Warick, Director of College Advancement**
  NorQuest College, Edmonton, AB

As a nonprofit housing developer, our biggest challenge was to get our message out to the community. Raising More Money showed us how to do the outreach and create an inspiring one-hour Ask Event program that touched people who didn't really know us before. In just one year, we raised $300,000 with this system, and our donor base grew from 30 to 300 donors, dramatically increasing our visibility and our financial stability. We can't wait for our next Ask Event!

— **Joanne Kosciolek, Vice President, Fund Development & Communications Central Community Housing Trust, Minneapolis, MN**

We achieved a record-breaking success at our first Ask Event breakfast! The keys to our success were following the Raising More Money Model precisely and the coaching we received after the workshop. We are convinced that this fundraising approach will make it possible for us to build a very solid foundation of lifelong donors. If you follow the model exactly, believe us, you cannot fail.

— **Rev. Mr. John Ruscheinsky, Director Immaculate Heart Retreat Center, Spokane, WA**

During an era when nonprofit organizations like ours are facing massive government cuts, it's not melodramatic to state that the funds we raised at our first "Paving the Road Home" breakfast saved the lives of many homeless people seeking shelter in the record-cold winter of 2004. Thank you, Raising More Money, for giving us the tools we needed to make this happen!

— **Gretchen Arntz, Chief Development Officer Emmaus, Inc., Haverhill, MA**

Our first Ask Event breakfast raised $305,000 from an event with 112 total guests! We gained many new donors and solidified our connections with prior donors. The event allowed students from our school to share their stories, and guests were thrilled with the content of the program and the length—just one hour! We now have much greater community support for our school, and our staff and board are fully convinced of the value of the Raising More Money system.

— **Jennifer Jordan, Development Director The Graham School, Columbus, OH**

The Raising More Money Model is one amazingly effective system! It allows all staff, volunteers, and other supporters to become a part of the success of our mission. In our first year using the model we saw immediate results that we have been able to build on year after year.
— **Katie Porta, President**
   Quest, Inc., Apopka, FL

It is hard to imagine that we would touch people, many who knew our organization only in general terms, so deeply in one hour that they would commit more than $80,000 to our mission. We received unanimous feedback that every detail of our Ask Event contributed to a complete experience that exceeded expectations and demanded a response. We are grateful that we had the Raising More Money program to follow and have become true believers in its power.
— **Ron Gregg, Co-Executive Director**
   Washtenaw Affordable Nonprofit Housing Corp., Ann Arbor, MI

The Raising More Money Model, and especially the Ask Event, completely changed not just our organization's fundraising system, but the entire structure of our organization and our thinking. We are very mission-focused now, and so are our donors! We are really touching people in our community, and this has resulted in many new donors, volunteers, board members, and even media coverage and publicity for our work.
— **Patricia Kemerling, Executive Director**
   The Arc, San Francisco, CA

Our Ask Event turned out to be a dream come true. We raised $360,000 at a one-hour event with 270 guests! The formula works!
— **Scot Adams, Executive Director**
   Catholic Charities, Omaha, NE

We have a small staff of 16 teachers and administrators, and before we did our first Ask Event, fundraising was only tolerated as a necessary evil. After the Ask Event, they were so moved and proud that they contributed over $15,000 in gifts and pledges, and they also became significant advocates and supporters outside the school. I increased my development staff overnight!"
— **Greg Meenahan, Development Director**
   Thomas Edison High School, Portland, OR

RAISING MORE M●NEY

THE
ASK EVENT
HANDBOOK

TERRY AXELROD

Raising More Money
The Ask Event Handbook
Terry Axelrod

Raising More Money Publications, Seattle, Washington
The following trademarks appear throughout this book:
Raising More Money Model®, Raising More Money E-New$®,
Raising More Money 101®, Next Step®,
Point of Entry™, and Treasure Map™

ISBN 0-9700455-3-0
LOC 2004109447

ATTENTION CORPORATIONS, UNIVERSITIES,
COLLEGES, AND PROFESSIONAL ORGANIZATIONS:
Quantity discounts are available on bulk purchases
of this book for educational purposes.
Special books or book excerpts can also be created to fit specific needs.
For information, please contact:
Raising More Money Publications
2100 North Pacific Street
Seattle, WA 98103
888-322-9357

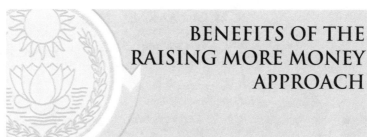

BENEFITS OF THE
RAISING MORE MONEY
APPROACH

- Gives your organization a system for tapping into the 84% of all contributions that come from individuals

- Focuses on fundraising as a science, rather than an art

- Continuously builds your base of lifelong donors; gets you off the treadmill

- Allows your organization to establish a multi-year unrestricted giving society

- Mission-based; honors your donors' true commitment to your work

- Includes everything you are already doing right

- Treats donors the way you would want to be treated:

  - Permission-based; no more strong-arming

  - Organic; allows time for donors to become educated, inspired, and involved before being asked for money

Also by Terry Axelrod:

Raising More Money—
A Step-by-Step Guide to Building Lifelong Donors
and
Raising More Money—
The Point of Entry Handbook

ACKNOWLEDGMENTS

This book is dedicated, first, to the over 1,000 organizations who have sent teams to our two-day Raising More Money Workshops, where we customize our model to the unique work of each group. Thank you for being willing to step off the funding "treadmill" and adopt a new approach to building sustainable funding for the mission of your organization from lifelong individual donors, and especially for doing the work it takes to implement this model. The results spoken of on the pages that follow do not occur without dedication, focus, and hard work. While I know, in the end, the results have been a source of great joy and satisfaction to each of your groups, the process is often grueling and takes real patience and courage as you bring everyone along. Without your dedication to the organizations that will benefit from these increased funds, we would not have such incredible successes to brag about or the tried-and-true formulas and templates shared in this book.

Next, this book is dedicated to our exceptional Raising More Money coaches for their tireless commitment to the success of each group they support through the process of implementing the entire model, including the Ask Event. My inbox is filled with letters of gratitude from coaching groups so deeply appreciative of your skill and caring in teaching them to tell their stories powerfully, rehearsing their key speakers, and tending to every detail to ensure these consistent, outstanding results. Thank you for demonstrating the spirit of contribution and abundance we strive to impart to all of our groups as they begin the process of building sustainable funding for the missions of their organizations. I know that the nearly $100 million dollars that has been raised to date by groups using the model—not to mention the increased community support for their work—would never have happened without each of you. I remember the pride you shared when we heard about the board member who got up on the table and danced with joy at the end of one group's Ask Event. In that same way, you are each group's biggest cheerleader.

Acknowledgments also to the staff in our Seattle home office for living and breathing the model so passionately every day and especially to our gifted young editor, Elizabeth Warden, for tirelessly guiding each step of the process in getting this book to the printer and ultimately to each of our readers. The steady hand and clear focus of senior editor Ann Overton were invaluable as well.

Finally to my family, and especially to the President of Raising More Money, my husband Alan Axelrod, for his unwavering support in every step of the process, always.

TABLE OF CONTENTS

SO YOU WANT TO
HAVE AN ASK EVENT?

I have put off writing this book for nearly eight years. Regardless of whether you have ever heard of the Raising More Money Model, the idea of putting on a Free One-Hour Ask Event is very seductive. The opportunity to gather a large group of people for one hour to focus on the mission of your organization and then generate multiple-year pledges for operational funding is more than most dedicated staff and board members can resist, especially when this event has the power of raising several million dollars. But the old reality, hand-to-mouth, "let's just make this year's goal and let the next person worry about next year" mentality is so entrenched that I have hesitated to write this book.

As long as the context in which the Ask Event is held is one of scarcity and survival, this elegant, simple, abundance-based model for building sustainable funding from lifelong individual donors will never fully take hold in an organization. In that environment, this four-step process, which is designed to take organizations off of the treadmill of direct mail, grant-writing, and—yes—special events, and into the world of abundant major gifts, will not prevail. Rather than leaving the legacy of a system that, like the source of a stream, continually generates lifelong donors, you will have left the legacy of the new hot event. In two or three short years, the "creativity" process will set in among people who never understood the broader context in which the Ask Event is designed to be used. The rationale behind each element of the Ask Event will have been lost. Rather than focusing on growing and ripening the fruit, in their desperation, people will pick any fruit in sight, leaving the whole process barren.

Before you launch into this blindly, I recommend you take to heart the following cautions:

1. Look at your deeper motivations for putting on this event. For most people who care about a nonprofit organization, special events have traditionally been a way to save the day, bring in some fast money, look like a hero, and then get back to the real work of fulfilling the organization's mission. If this type of short-term, "treadmill" thinking characterizes your reason for wanting to put on an Ask Event, you should definitely not proceed; rather, you should continue with the successful events, such as golf tournaments or galas, that your group has been doing to date. People are accustomed to attending those types of events, paying a ticket price, perhaps purchasing an item in your silent auction, and going home feeling they have attended a nice "fundraiser."

The Free One-Hour Ask Event is *not* another stand-alone special event for your staff and volunteers to add to the list. It is the third step of a four-step, circular model for building lifelong donors who will provide sustainable funding for your organization's mission. In other words, the Ask Event is part of a comprehensive system.

2. Look at your own long-term commitment to the organization considering putting on this Ask Event. On a scale of 1-10, how passionate are you about their work? How long do you see yourself being involved there? Are you willing to do the work it will take to alter the course of fundraising there forever?

I know this may sound a bit extreme. After all, you may be new to the organization or may have several nonprofit groups you might like to try this with. But you need to step into this with your eyes open. **The Raising More Money Model is a major shift from the old hand-to-mouth, one-year-at-a-time, scarcity-based "treadmill"** fundraising mentality to a rational, abundance-based system. Although that sounds like something most groups want theoretically, they often are not willing to make such a major change in practice. People—even good people like you and me—tend to resist change. If you are planning to be the champion of this model for your organization, you will, in all likelihood, encounter significant resistance for a long period of time. If you see your involvement with this organization as short-term (less than two years), you should not proceed. Systemic change takes time.

3. Read my first book, *Raising More Money—A Step-by-Step Guide to Building Lifelong Donors*. In the few hours it will take you, you will get a far deeper appreciation for the entire model and the role the Ask Event plays in the process.

4. Put together a team. Do not think you can be the exceptional person who pulls this off alone. We have had many other Raising More Money "devotees" who have gone to great lengths to put on stellar Ask Events, single-handedly. As wonderful as that one event may turn out, it rarely lives on at the organization. Three years later, the organization has either heavily modified the format or switched to an old-style fundraising event.

To be successful in the long term, you must have a team of four to six people—board, staff, and volunteers—who truly understand the larger implications of the model and are not just "helping out" by putting on your new exciting event. If this event is perceived as Sally's or Bill's new wild idea for an event, it is destined for a short lifespan and you will have missed the whole point of this model.

Take the time to get people on board with the entire Raising More Money Model. Choose your team carefully. Select long-term players—people with a deep dedication to the mission. That way, as natural attrition occurs, there will be ongoing champions among the board, staff, and volunteers to carry on the plan.

Much as everyone loves a superstar, in the nonprofit world, without a team, you have little chance of leaving any kind of legacy.

5. Do not skip over doing Point of Entry Events. Use *Raising More Money—The Point of Entry Handbook* to help you customize yours. Design a great Point of Entry Event and put one on at least monthly. If you are not doing Point of Entry Events at least monthly, you are not really using the Raising More Money Model. These Point of Entry Events will be your real legacy. With all the glitz and focus on the money, and the temptation to pick the fruit too early, people forget that they need to tend and water the tree. Your Point of Entry is that tree; it will keep the entire program self-sustaining. Twenty years from now, if you are to be remembered for anything at your organization, have it be for that inspiring one-hour tour or meeting that everyone in your community still invites people to attend.

6. Don't pressure anyone to do this. As soon as board members hear a new event is on the horizon, they may retreat to either "I hate fundraising" or "I've already asked all my friends." You need to treat your board members just as you would treat brand-new guests at a Point of Entry and slowly bring them through the process. Don't assume that just because they are on your board, your organization's mission is their number one passion. Even if it once was their true passion, it may have grown stale in the face of day-to-day board life.

The same is true of your staff. Program staff have their own jobs to do. At best, if they will be supportive of your efforts, move forward. Even a hint of "we need you to get on board with this" will add an air of desperation that will ultimately backfire. Instead, share your excitement about this more mission-centered approach to fundraising and ask for their input in designing your Essential Story.

7. Come to our two-day Raising More Money 101 Workshop with your team. Let our highly-skilled instructors and coaches work with you to customize and implement this system for sustaining the mission of your organization through lifelong individual donors. Your group of six—often reluctant—souls will be transformed into an inspired and focused fundraising team. They will understand and appreciate the deeper impact of sticking with the entire model. In the year of follow-up coaching that is included in the workshop, we

can approve every detail of your program, scripts, printed materials, and pledge levels, and we can even rehearse your Ask Event speakers. Having tracked results closely, we know that the investment in attending our workshop pays for itself many times over.

8. Finally, I recommend that you take a deeper look at the legacy you are committed to leaving this organization. Consider the possibility that you could leave the legacy of a system that generates sustainable funding for the mission of your organization from lifelong donors—donors who truly understand the value of this organization's work and are not giving because they have been tricked, strong-armed, manipulated, or made to feel guilty, but because they are dedicated to the fulfillment of the organization's mission.

Think for a moment about your own charitable giving. We each have our own short list of what I call our "default charities." These are the groups we give to in good times or bad. Why is that? What is it about each of these organizations that gets us to give and feel great about it? There is almost always some deeper connection to their work, often a personal connection. I still give every year to a search and rescue team that airlifted my sister out of the mountains when she got lost on a hiking trip many years ago. Perhaps one of your friends or family members had that disease this organization is working to eradicate. It may be your alma mater or faith organization.

In every case, it is a group you choose to give to; you actually *want* to be giving to this organization because you so value their work.

This is what you are committing to if you take on the Ask Event. You are implementing the third step in a four-step circular process for positioning your organization on the short list of more and more individual donors who truly care about your mission and are giving to you for the right reasons.

Having said all that, I will consider you forewarned. Best of luck as you lead your organization into the new abundance-based fundraising reality.

BEFORE YOU BEGIN

CHAPTER 1

PUTTING THE ASK EVENT IN CONTEXT: THE RAISING MORE MONEY MODEL

If this book is your first introduction to the Raising More Money Model, welcome to the world of mission-centered fundraising from individuals. If you are already familiar with the model, welcome back. Whether you know the ins and outs of Ask Events or are just learning about this event for the first time, it is essential to position this Free One-Hour Ask Event in your mind as one way to accomplish Step Three: Asking for Money, and to remember that this is just one of four essential steps in this circular model.

Let's back up then and put the Ask Event in the broader context of the entire model.

The Raising More Money Model is a four-step system for building sustainable funding for the mission of your organization from lifelong individual donors. It works for all types of nonprofits, large and small, urban and rural, national and international, with all types of missions. This is a bridge strategy for moving organizations from the transactional world of direct mail, grant-writing, and special events into the relationship-oriented world of major gifts, planned gifts, and endowments. The model provides a step-by-step recipe for success. And, as with any cherished family recipe, you do not want to experiment with the formula. This is not the time for creativity; just follow the recipe.

Even if you are familiar with this approach, I recommend you read the description of the model again, to remind yourself of each step. This time, read with a focus on where the Ask Event takes place in the cycle—at Step Three, after potential donors have attended a Point of Entry Event, been followed up with, cultivated, and are ready to give.

IT'S A CIRCLE

The model is designed as a circle. Imagine a loop, a closed circuit, or an old-fashioned electric train set that goes around and around. Once your potential donors get on board, they stay on board. The cycle starts over each time they give. Your job is to tailor this model to your organization and to keep expanding it to include as many people as possible, year after year.

The model has four essential steps, which take you through the cycle.

Step One: The Point of Entry

Potential donors get on the track at a Point of Entry. The Point of Entry is a one-hour introductory event that educates and inspires people about your organization. You do not ask for money at a Point of Entry Event. You should assume that every potential donor will attend only one Point of Entry Event in their lifetime, so it should be memorable.

A Point of Entry must include three components:

1. The basic information—the "Facts 101" about your organization, including the vision and needs.

2. An "Emotional Hook" so compelling people will never forget it.

3. A system for "Capturing the Names," including addresses, phone numbers, and e-mail addresses of the guests, with their permission.

Your Point of Entry must give people a sense of how the work of your organization changes lives. That is because, as individuals, we are emotional donors looking for rational reasons to justify our emotional decision to give. Your Point of Entry Event must satisfy both the head and the heart; neither the emotion nor the facts alone will do it. The Point of Entry must intertwine facts and emotion so that, before they even realize it, the guests are satisfied. If you don't accomplish both, you won't have a foundation from which to launch a relationship with a lifelong donor.

The Facts 101 consist of:

- A brief history of the organization.
- A basic statement of the programs and services offered.
- The numbers: people served, budget size, etc.
- The vision for the future, including a clear statement of what you will need to get to that point. You have to clearly identify the gap. You can easily do this while highlighting your strengths. "As wonderful as this program is, there are still 2,000 children in our area going unserved." "With just three more computers we could increase our efficiency immensely and spend more time serving people."

The Emotional Hook is most easily conveyed through stories, which may be presented in-person by a staff member, family member, or the actual person who benefited from your programs or services. Once you have identified the most representative story that is sure to capture people's emotions every time, you can tell this "Essential Story" and others like it using a variety of methods: a video or audio tape, a letter, a tour, or a dramatic or artistic presentation.

Finally, you must be sure you have a permission-based system to Capture the Names, addresses, phone numbers, and e-mail addresses of every guest. After all, if the Point of Entry Event is just the first point in a cycle of lifelong giving, you will need to know how to contact each person again. Rather than tricking or manipulating them by pretending to collect their business cards for some other purpose, you can ask people to fill out a card with their contact information, because they have been told in advance what to expect. They know they are coming to a brief introductory session to learn about a wonderful organization. They know that they will not be asked to give money at the Point of Entry. They are coming because they have been invited personally by a friend or someone they trust.

Step Two: Follow Up and Involve

When people are invited to your organization's Point of Entry Events, they are told the truth: that you are trying to spread the word about your work and solicit feedback about your programs from people in your community. After all, that is exactly what you are trying to do. However, the only way you will know what they really thought about your organization or your Point of Entry Event is if you ask them. If you are not planning on doing a rigorous job of following up with each and every person who attends a Point of Entry Event, there is no point in having these events at all. In fact, the very first step in planning each event should be to design your follow-up system.

Therefore, the second step on the circle of a self-sustaining individual giving program is making a personal Follow-Up Call within a week to each person who attended the Point of Entry Event.

The Follow-Up Call is not a standard thank you, for which a note would suffice. It is an interactive research call. Think of it as a one-on-one focus group in which you gather critical data on each potential lifelong donor and friend. The purpose of this call is to generate an authentic dialog with true give-and-take. If you think of the people with whom you have lifelong relationships—your friends and family—you will realize that these relationships are rooted in a true dialog. It should be no different with your donors.

The Follow-Up Call must be made by someone your guests met at the Point of Entry, not by a stranger. This call follows a specific, five-point format that will help you get the information you need.

Point One

"Thank you for coming." You certainly need to thank them. They are busy people who did not have to take the time to come to your Point of Entry Event.

Point Two

Ask: "What did you think (of the tour, the organization, the issue)?" Ask enough questions to get them talking.

Point Three

Listen. This is the hardest step for most of us, and by far the most critical component of the Follow-Up Call. Stop talking and listen. In this model, the more you listen, the more you will notice that potential donors are telling you exactly how they would like to become involved with your organization. If you are too busy talking or planning what you want to say next, you will miss all the rich cues.

Point Four

If they have not already told you, ask: "Is there any way you could see yourself becoming involved with our organization?" You let them tell you. In the new reality of donor-centered individual giving, the donors have their own ideas—ideas that may not mesh with your needs. You still need to listen and be open to saying yes to what they offer.

Point Five

Finally, ask: "Is there anyone else you think we should invite to a _____ (Point of Entry Event)?" You may be surprised to discover that, because you have taken the time to listen at each step along the way, people will be so appreciative they will naturally suggest others you should contact. Even people who are honest enough to tell you that your issue is not their hot button will have other people for you to invite. Ask if they would mind if you contact these people directly and use their name. Then do it.

Every bit of data you gather should be recorded in your database. Be sure your computer system has a good section for you to record notes about each contact with each donor.

Letting People Off the Hook

In the follow-up process, you are sure to come across people who are not interested in getting more involved with your organization. The Follow-Up Call is where you can let them off the hook. Don't even think about taking it personally. Put yourself in their shoes. They took the time to come to the Point of Entry Event. Yes, they were touched and impressed with what you do; they may even send you a little check as a courtesy. But they are deeply involved in another cause that is their true passion. While they like you and know that you are doing good work, you are never going to make it to the top third of their giving list.

Let these people go graciously. "Bless and release" them. Thank them sincerely for taking the time to come. If they are open enough to mention the other issue or organization they are involved with, compliment it. Honor their commitment and dedication to that cause. Do not offer to send them an envelope they can use to make a small gift. Let them completely off the hook. It will disarm them and distinguish you from the others. Think of how grateful you would feel if people heard you the first time when you really meant "No."

In the long run, these people will help you in many ways, primarily by referring others. Many times, people have told me, "This type of program just isn't my thing. I'm deeply involved in another organization, and that's where I want to be putting my resources right now." Then, when I asked them the final question about others they know who might want to come to a Point of Entry Event, they would often say, "You should definitely call my wife (or my work colleague or my friend). This is exactly the kind of thing they'd be interested in. Tell them I recommend they come out and take your tour." What better compliment than for a person to refer you to others and encourage you to use their name? In the long run, you will have made a real friend, just by letting someone off the hook.

Remember, this is a model for building lifelong donors—donors who are so interested in your mission that they want to stay with you for the long term. It is as if, one by one, you are selecting the people who are going to be part of your organization's family forever. You do not want to select someone who is not really interested. There are so many generous and caring folks who truly understand and appreciate the value of what you are doing. They are the ones you are on a scouting mission to find.

The Cultivation Superhighway

Where we are headed in the model is along the path to the third step, where the donor will be asked for money. Notice you have not done that at either Step One, the Point of Entry Event, or at Step Two, the Follow-Up Call. You have been busy warming up and screening people to see if they would make loyal lifelong donors. In our model, by the time you get around to asking for money, you should be certain that the person is ready to give.

In the old reality, the "Ask" often happened too soon, before the person had a chance to fully buy in, head and heart, to the mission of the organization. In the new reality, there is no need for that. In fact, if you have any sense that the person may not be ready to give, don't ask yet. Trust your instincts and hold off until you know they are ready.

Asking is very much like picking the ripe, low-hanging fruit from a tree. When a person first comes to your Point of Entry Event, they are brand-new to your organization, completely unripened fruit. By going through the tour, they begin to ripen, and with the Follow-Up Call they ripen further. By the time you get around to asking them for money, it should be nothing more than "nudging the inevitable"—like easily picking a piece of fruit off a tree the moment it is ready. On the other hand, if you wait too long, what happens? The fruit becomes overripe, falls to the ground and spoils. In other words, in the life cycle of each donor, there are perfect moments for asking for money. You have to tune your radar to those moments.

In this model, everything along the path between Step Two, the Follow-Up Call, and Step Three, the Ask, is called the Cultivation Superhighway. The more contacts you have with a potential donor along the Superhighway, the more money they will give you when you ask. There is a direct correlation between the number of contacts and the size of the gifts received.

This should come as no surprise. Again, think of yourself as that donor. Imagine that an organization had already taken the time to educate you and follow up personally. The more you heard from a real person at that organization directly and the more specifically their calls, e-mails, faxes, or meetings with you related to your particular needs, the more inclined you would be to give a larger gift the next time they asked.

It is worth considering what qualifies as a contact. Is it mailing a potential donor your newsletter or invitations to upcoming events? Yes, those do count as contacts, but nothing substitutes for a person-to-person, live contact. The best of these contacts are dictated by the donor. If they are generous enough in the Follow-Up Call to tell you how they might like to become more involved, your job is to stay in contact with them to make those things happen. Keep following up; keep giving them feedback.

If, for example, they would like to help you start a new program you would love to have, you will need to invite them back to meet with the key staff in that area, with the board, or with the director. Or there may be other folks from the community that the potential donor would also like to involve. Having them invite others to find out about your organization at a Point of Entry Event is also a key indicator of their support.

If you have done your homework and tended to their needs and interests throughout all of your contacts with them, this person will become a self-proclaimed volunteer for your organization. While their "project" may not fit into your normal job description for a volunteer, in the new reality of raising funds from individuals this person is a volunteer with a customized, self-designed job description.

According to *Giving and Volunteering in the United States*, 84% of all charitable contributions come from households in which one or more family members volunteer. In other words, being a volunteer is a key indicator of giving. While the research doesn't specify that volunteers give to the same organizations where they volunteer their time, it does show that giving and involvement go hand-in-hand. And in the new reality of individual giving, you should assume that giving will follow involvement, in whatever way the donor defines involvement.

Donors need to know that you need them and that their contribution will make a difference in accomplishing your mission. They need to know that you are responsive to their suggestions. In many cases, they need to know that you need them for more than their money. For these reasons, the more meaningful your contacts with these people are, the better. Contacts are what ripen the fruit.

Step Three: Asking for Money

When the donor is ready to be asked, the first thing to consider is the medium you will use. Will you ask in-person, over the telephone, online, at an event, or by mail? Any of these is acceptable, although, generally speaking, the bigger the gift you will ask for, the more successful you will be if you ask face-to-face and one-on-one.

There are two ways to ask for money in our model, either one-on-one in-person, or at the Free One-Hour Ask Event. If you have taken many people through your Point of Entry Events in a short span of time, then followed up and involved them to their satisfaction, you may well find yourself in the enviable position of having many people to ask for a contribution at about the same time. In that case, the Free One-Hour Ask Event, the subject of this book, is ideal. The critical mass of true believers in the same room will produce remarkable results in just an hour.

On the other hand, if people have been trickling through your Point of Entry Events more slowly, or if you are starting with Points of Re-Entry for prior donors, you may do better asking one-on-one, either in-person or by phone.

Regardless of the venue, in our model, every Ask must include two essential ingredients.

Multiple-Year Pledges

The first essential ingredient in asking for money is that you ask people to become part of a Multiple-Year Giving Society by making a multiple-year pledge to support the unrestricted operating needs of the organization. That's right, you ask them to commit at the time of their first pledge to give that same amount each year for a specified number of years. Why? Not for the reason you may think. As wonderful as it is for your organization to know you have the stability of all those pledges waiting to be collected each year, that is not the main reason for asking for multiple-year pledges.

The main reason is for the donor. It allows donors to declare themselves as part of your organization's family. It gives a particular group of more committed donors the opportunity to say: "You can count on me. I'm a long-term believer in what you are up to."

Think for a moment about your own giving. Make a mental list of all the places you have been supporting over the years, getting relatively little feedback in return. What if someone from one of those organizations was to call you and say: "Hello, Ms. Jones, we notice you have been a loyal donor for the last fifteen years. Thank you for your support. We are calling to ask if you would be willing to make a pledge to give at that same gift level for the next five years." You would have a hard time saying no, right? After all, you would probably keep giving there anyway.

The value of a Multiple-Year Giving Society is that it allows donors to "go public" with their commitment and support. Most of us are very private in our giving. We just keep sending in our little (or not so little) check year after year. We are not looking for recognition. We each have our personal reasons for giving. We don't even talk about our giving with others. The satisfaction of giving is often more than enough.

By making a multiple-year pledge, we know that our name will be listed in the Multiple-Year Giving Society. Others may notice. Moreover, it gives us license to talk about our fondness for this organization with those close to us—family and friends, the people we trust, respect, and confide in. Our natural tendency as people who have made that multiple-year commitment is to share our enthusiasm with others.

Units of Service

When asking for multiple-year pledges, it is crucial to specify the levels of contribution. We call these Units of Service. They are the giving levels, gift clubs—gimmicks, if you will. They are the bite-sized chunks of unrestricted funding that one person can support. They relate to the needs that were clearly identified at the Point of Entry Event and at every contact along the way.

You do not need more than three Units of Service, and there should be a significant gap in their dollar levels. In the new reality, the lowest level will be $1,000 a year (or about $83 a month). Many people who truly love your work and want to be lifelong members of your organization's family can and will give at that level. In fact, many may already be giving at that level when you total up their many gifts each year.

The key thing to know is that these levels are gimmicks, and in the new reality of lifelong donors, it is fine to tell people that. If they have bought into your mission fully, they will trust you to use the money for the overall programs of the organization. They know that someone has to pay the light bill and the salaries. They know they can look at your annual audit if they want to see exactly how the money was spent.

Step Four: Introducing Others; Reconnecting Existing Donors

In the fourth step of the model, individual members of the Multiple-Year Giving Society introduce others to your organization by inviting them to Point of Entry Events. Since your donors have been through the cycle with you, they know you will take good care of their friends. You will educate and inspire them at the Point of Entry, follow up personally, involve them as appropriate, or let them off the hook graciously if they are not interested. Your Multiple-Year Donors will trust the organization to treat their friends with respect. Their secret hope, of course, is that their friends will fall in love with your organization too—in their own right, for their own reasons—and become lifelong donors as well. This step completes the first circuit around the model for a brand-new donor.

Free Feel-Good Cultivation Events: Points of Re-Entry

To keep your donors in the cycle, every Multiple-Year Giving Society Donor is invited to one or two Free Feel-Good Cultivation Events during the year—also called Point of Re-Entry Events. As the name implies, these events serve to reconnect them to the facts and emotion of your work. Donors are encouraged to invite others to Free Feel-Good Cultivation/Point of Re-Entry Events. For these new guests, this event will be their Point of Entry. For the prior donors, the event serves to reinforce their wise investment in your organization and to deepen their interest and commitment.

These Free Feel-Good Cultivation Events can be regularly scheduled events having to do with the work of the organization, such as a graduation of your program's participants or a lecture on a topic of interest, or they can be events planned specially for these donors. You may even choose to have different events for donors at different levels.

Following each Free Feel-Good Cultivation/Point of Re-Entry Event, every donor receives another one-on-one Follow-Up Call asking a few more open-ended questions and giving the donor the opportunity to offer suggestions for names of others to be invited to a Point of Entry Event. This in turn leads to more cultivation, more involvement, and deeper and deeper permission and trust. Whatever they tell you in each Follow-Up Call determines the frequency and quality of involvement this particular donor would like to have, including the timing of the next Ask.

After the next gift is received, another Follow-Up Call is made to say thank you, there is more conversation, and on it goes. All the while, you are looking and listening for how else they might want to become involved. You may even consider inviting them to take on a leadership role in a key volunteer or board position, as appropriate.

Ideally, in the course of the year, you will have three or four occasions for personal, one-on-one contact with each donor. This contact can be made by your lead development staff person or other key staff, or by one of your volunteer Donor Service Representatives (akin to a customer service representative in a bank) who is assigned to that donor for at least two years at a time. These contacts are nothing intrusive or artificial, but rather a natural give-and-take, either triggered by gifts received or by their participation in one of your Free Feel-Good Cultivation Events.

Thus, the simple circle becomes a spiral, with an ever-growing number of Multiple-Year Donors.

CHAPTER 2

CONVERTING EXISTING EVENTS TO THE RAISING MORE MONEY MODEL

Now that you have an overview of the model, let's look at how you can convert many of your more labor-intensive, stand-alone special events into events that can forward your system for building sustainable funding from lifelong donors.

The purpose of this section on events is for you to be able to do just that—to categorize and redesign, if necessary, each of your events so that they fit together into a carefully crafted system of annual events which you can leave as a legacy for your organization. Please be forewarned: over time, adopting the Raising More Money approach is likely to grow deeper relationships with your donors and put an end to many of your one-year-at-a-time, "fundraising fluff" special events.

Before we can decide how to convert many of your existing events, we need to step back and review the Raising More Money classification of events. In this model for building a self-sustaining individual giving program, any event your organization is now putting on can be recast to fit into one of the following four categories:

- A Point of Entry Event
- A Point of Entry Conversion Event
- A Free One-Hour Ask Event
- A Free Feel-Good Cultivation Event (also known as a Point of Re-Entry)

Start by making a list of all the events your organization currently puts on each year. Include all types of events: annual dinners, holiday parties, volunteer and donor recognition events, anniversary events, golf tournaments, walk-a-thons, theater events, black tie galas, auctions, etc. You can even include volunteer recruitment events, training classes, or actual performances of your arts organization.

CONVERTING YOUR CURRENT EVENTS

Now let's define the four types of events you could convert them to.

Point of Entry Events

The first type of event is the Point of Entry—that generic repeatable event you could leave as a legacy to your organization. Imagine if you could actually take some of the events you are now working diligently to produce and turn them into your regularly scheduled Point of Entry Events. Without having to invent a whole new series of events, you could jump-start your Point of Entry program quickly.

By now, you are familiar with the three essential ingredients of our stand-alone Point of Entry Event: Facts 101, the Emotional Hook, and being able to Capture the Names of the guests with their permission. Guests who attend these events are usually invited word-of-mouth by a friend and are coming for the sole purpose of learning more about your organization. The content of this introductory session is so generic you could put it in a box and take it to someone's home or office, in addition to presenting it at your own site.

Think about which of your existing events may already meet these requirements or could easily be modified to do so. The best contenders are well-attended, program-related events that repeat weekly or monthly; for example, tours, orientations, or open houses you may offer for new volunteers, staff, or members. Odds are, with only a bit of tweaking, you could have a ready-made Point of Entry.

The one criterion that is trickiest to meet is that the guests need to know in advance that they are coming to an introductory session about your organization, as opposed to coming to a more specific volunteer training, lecture on a particular topic, or an open house. For example, a retirement home we worked with had been holding regular Sunday afternoon open houses for family members and potential new residents. After adopting the Raising More Money Model, it was easy for them to add a thirty-minute sit-down Point of Entry "meeting." Rather than having to organize a whole new set of events, they merely added (and publicized) this more formal component to an already popular and well-attended event in their community.

No doubt, your organization also has existing events that could qualify as natural Point of Entry Events, with only minor modifications.

Point of Entry Conversion Events

The second type of event is what we call a Point of Entry Conversion Event. Distinct from the standard Point of Entry, these conversion events are usually the ones we call "fundraisers." It is fine to charge people money to come to a Point of Entry Conversion Event; just be sure that all of the objectives of a standard Point of Entry have been covered before they leave.

Here is a little test to see whether your event qualifies as a Point of Entry for your guests: The next day, if someone had asked them about the dinner-dance or the golf tournament, could the guests have answered the following two-question pop quiz?

> *Question 1: What was the name of the organization for which the event was raising funds?*
> While they may well remember how much they enjoyed the golf or the dinner-dance, will they be able to recall the name of the organization that worked so hard to produce the event and ultimately received their financial support?

> *Question 2: What does that organization do?*
> Even if your name is well known in your community, do not assume that people truly know about the breadth of your programs. What people will remember most is a video or short testimonial from someone who has benefited from your work.

In other words, you will need to insert a Point of Entry element into the sit-down portion of your fundraising event. This should include a short Visionary Leader Talk with facts and emotion plus a brief, live testimonial from a person whose life has been changed thanks to the work of your organization. With good preparation, this can all be accomplished in ten minutes.

It almost goes without saying that you also need to Capture the Names with the guests' permission. At most of these events, such as auctions or golf tournaments, you will have a natural way to know who will be coming in advance. Do not assume that this means you have their permission to follow up with them after the event.

Do you have good records of the names and phone numbers of the guests? Moreover, would you have a legitimate reason for calling them after the event to find out what they thought of it? Or would that seem too contrived? What could you add to the event that would let those guests who might want more information identify themselves so you would have sufficient permission to follow up with them?

For that explicit permission, you need to ask people at some point during the event if they would like you to contact them. The easiest way to do this is by placing a card under their lunch or dinner plate or in the center of their table. The emcee needs to refer to the card and encourage people to fill it out and leave it with their table host if they would like to speak directly with someone from the organization.

Free One-Hour Ask Events

The third event is our Free One-Hour Ask Event. While other events may resemble this, most organizations are not yet actually doing the type of event we are referring to here.

To qualify as a Free One-Hour Ask Event in this model, the guests are invited personally to a free breakfast or lunch event by a friend who serves as a Table Captain.

The guests know in advance that they will be asked to give money at the event. The Table Captain also must be sure to inform them at the point of the invitation that there is "no minimum and no maximum gift" expected. As much as anything, they are being asked to come and learn more about the organization. It will be the organization's job to inspire and educate them so they will want to give.

The Free One-Hour Ask Event is ideally suited to the new fundraising reality because it provides a straightforward, time-limited advertisement of the outstanding work of your organization. In one tightly choreographed hour, this event provides the Facts, the Emotional Hook, and a compelling Ask for multiple-year support at specific giving levels.

This event is an extremely effective money raiser for the following reasons:

1. Many of the guests have already attended a "real" Point of Entry Event, received a Follow-Up Call, and have been personally involved. They serve as a critical mass within the larger group and provide a momentum towards giving.

2. The guests have been well prepared in advance and know that making a contribution will be optional at the event. You must base your financial projections on the assumption that only half of the guests will give at all. Then you may be pleasantly surprised.

3. The event is free. In fundraising, "free" is magical. If you were to charge even $10 a person to attend this event, it would never be as successful. At an Ask Event, people are given a nice, basic breakfast or lunch, for which they do not feel overly obligated. They are free to enjoy themselves and to give freely when asked, if they so choose. Do not do this event as a dinner. Dinner implies a greater degree of obligation, which could get in the way of donors choosing how much they would like to give.

While it may be tempting, I do not recommend converting an existing event to a Free One-Hour Ask Event. It tends to upset people, especially if the event has been taking place for many years and people are accustomed to its format. The subtleties of the Free One-Hour Ask Event will be disconcerting to people. Far better to start with a fresh event, ideally in the opposite season of the year, and have it become highly successful. Then you can decide what else to do with the older event; perhaps find a sponsor to cover the costs and convert it to the fourth type of event, a Free Feel-Good Cultivation Event.

Free Feel-Good Cultivation Events
(also known as Points of Re-Entry)

Fourth, and finally, comes the Free Feel-Good Cultivation Event. The name pretty much says it all. These are the "reward" events for your Multiple-Year Giving Society Donors that reconnect them to the Emotional Hook and reinforce the wisdom of their investment in your organization. That means these events always include a program or theme that ties to your mission.

Do not underestimate the magic of a "free" event. If you inspire them, people will remember you gave them something for free when it comes time to ask them for the next contribution. Just make sure you have one or more underwriters who receive plenty of credit, so your loyal donors will know you did not spend any of their money to pay for this event.

To keep it simple, you can invite donors to internal events already planned to honor your clients or families, such as graduations, show-and-tell nights, special theater performances, or expert lectures. Many of the events you now have that are free to your guests—donor or volunteer recognition events, awards ceremonies, or graduations—will fall into this category.

Unlike Point of Entry Conversion Events, these Free Feel-Good Cultivation Events are not intended to attract new friends to the organization, but rather to cultivate your inner circle of Multiple-Year Donors. These events are aimed at prior donors in appreciation of their loyal support. They powerfully reconnect donors to the mission of the organization and reinforce their original decision to give. Just as with a Point of Entry, the Point of Re-Entry or Free Feel-Good Cultivation Event gives people the Facts 101, the Emotional Hook, and a permission-based method for Capturing the Names. Donors leave feeling good, saying to themselves: "I'm glad I give money there. I will keep doing that. Maybe I could give more."

Of course, these insiders are always encouraged to bring friends to these Free Feel-Good Cultivation Events as well, so long as the focus of the event really is on your loyal prior donors. (For the new people, the event will be a Point of Entry Event. Just be sure to do the rigorous follow-up work that normally follows a Point of Entry Event.)

Free Feel-Good Cultivation Events can take on many forms. Most obvious are the traditional recognition events such as awards dinners, picnics, barbecues, or dinner parties in private homes. In a second category are the informal, but invitation-only, in-house program-related events, such as a special night for donors to serve soup in your soup kitchen or a special pre-graduation reception for Multiple-Year Giving Society Donors. In the third category are the formal or informal briefings or updates with a celebrity scientist or artist on their newest work or discovery.

These events can also be varied for donors at different giving levels. You may invite your biggest donors to an elegant dinner at the most exclusive private home or with a revered person in your field, if that is the sort of thing they would like. Your smaller Multiple-Year Donors might be invited to a dinner or lecture series, a family picnic, or a special "environmental day" or "peace day." Free Feel-Good Cultivation Events may also be used to introduce insiders to the next dream for the organization, especially a major gifts campaign or endowment.

Finally, just as with a Point of Entry Event, a Point of Re-Entry always engenders a Follow-Up Call, eliciting more feedback, which in turn enables you to further customize your approach to each donor. This keeps the donor going around the cycle with you.

Planning Your Free Feel-Good Cultivation Events Strategically

I recommend a minimum of one Free Feel-Good Cultivation Event per year, targeted to your Multiple-Year Giving Society members. In addition, it is a good idea to have a second event for all of your donors.

As for best times of year to hold these events, they are most often scheduled to occur about three months after your Ask Events or else to coincide with natural program events such as arts performances, graduations, and holiday celebrations.

DESIGNING YOUR SYSTEM OF EVENTS

Now that you understand the event classification within the Raising More Money Model, you should be ready to begin designing your system.

Using the following Converting Existing Events worksheet, list out all of your current events. Now make your plan for what type of event you would like to convert each of them into over time. Also begin to plot out on a calendar the ideal time of year for each event if you are starting from scratch.

CONVERTING EXISTING EVENTS

Current Events	Convert Event To:				Ideal Month	Convert By When
	Point of Entry	Point of Entry Conversion	Free Feel-Good Cultivation Event	Free One-Hour Ask Event		
1						
2						
3						
4						
5						
6						
7						
8						
9						
10						

Ultimately, what you are aiming to design is what we call a System of Events—a lasting set of events that build on each other throughout the year, providing each donor or potential donor with precisely the number and quality of contacts they would like.

For starters, I recommend the following: one Point of Entry Event per month, one Free One-Hour Ask Event per year (for the best time of year for this event, see page 66), two Free Feel-Good Cultivation Events per year (one for your Multiple-Year Giving Society Donors and the other for all your donors), and as few Point of Entry Conversion Events as possible. These Point of Entry Conversion Events, especially the ones that have been your most labor-intensive "fundraisers," should be thoroughly examined to determine which ones are worth the effort, and therefore should be sustained long-term as part of your system, and which ones should not.

Do not be discouraged in this process. It may take two to three years before you can rotate events to a different time of year or phase them out altogether. Your purpose now is to design the ideal System of Events for your organization.

All events should work together to support each other. For example, if you decide with your team that you will be putting on the Free One-Hour Ask Event every year in either the spring or fall, you will want your main Free Feel-Good Cultivation Event to take place in the next season. The first year, you might have more than one event crowded into the same season because you have already announced that date or had the invitations printed, but by next year you could rotate that event to another part of the year.

The time and thought you put into designing this System of Events will be well worth the effort.

CHAPTER 3

DECIDING WHETHER TO
HAVE AN ASK EVENT

You are now at a critical juncture. This event is sounding good. You understand that it is part of a larger model and that model makes sense to you. You can see that the event would work for your organization—*eventually.*

Here are the factors should you consider in deciding whether or not you are ready to put on the Free One-Hour Ask Event in the next year.

DECIDING FACTORS
How many people have attended your Points of Entry?

This should be your biggest concern. The success of the Ask Event will depend on having a minimum of 20% of the guests attend prior Point of Entry Events. We call this the 20% critical mass rule, and it is not hard to achieve. Furthermore, once you commit to putting on the event and select your Table Captains, you can begin our "backfill Point of Entry" strategy to help you exceed the 20% number. Of course, the higher the percentage of guests at your Ask Event who have been cultivated through the first two steps of the model, the better. Many groups we work with already know that 50-80% of their Ask Event guests have been cultivated sufficiently so that they arrive predisposed to giving.

How many people do you already know who would be happy to serve as Table Captains at the event and would be reliable enough to fill a table with ten people?

Note that there are two parts to this question. First, how many people would be happy to serve as Table Captains? That number may be significantly larger than those who could reliably fill a table of ten people. For most groups, it is tempting to choose Table Captains who have the most money or the best contacts. Keep in mind that the best determinant of a good Table Captain is passion. The people who are true believers in your work are the ones who are most likely to fulfill their role as Table Captains and bring people to the event who will in turn get involved for the right reason (their interest in your mission). Of course, some of these Table Captains will be the people with the best contacts and the most money, and some will not.

Can you schedule the event to take place in the next year?

It takes a minimum of six to nine months from the time you start having Point of Entry Events to the date of your first Ask Event. Is there a natural time in your organization's annual calendar of activities to schedule this event? The best times of the year to have the Ask Event are spring and late fall, ideally May or November, unless your event will take place in a community with many seasonal visitors or "snow birds." In that case, April is generally the best month for the Ask Event. Can you rotate or move any existing events and projects to allow the Ask Event to happen in one of the ideal months?

Will the outcomes of the event—financial or otherwise—be enough to make everyone happy?

This is a serious question to consider. For organizations that send teams of six people to our two-day workshops and then take advantage of the coaching through the process of putting on this event, the results are predictable. If 200 people attend the Ask Event, the event should raise approximately $100,000. However, that $100,000 includes five years' worth of multiple-year pledges, which means that the first year's income from the event could be as low as one-fifth of that $100,000, or $20,000. Some of our alumni groups find that their other special events are currently yielding more than that.

Of course, over time, assuming they continue with the entire model, the Free One-Hour Ask Event will keep generating at least $100,000 at each subsequent event, again spread out over five years of pledges, constantly multiplying the amount raised each year.

The following chart assumes that you put on an Ask Event of the same size for each of the next five years and that each year's event brings in a total of $100,000 ($20,000 a year for each of the next five years). You can see that by the fifth year, you will be receiving $100,000 in pledges.

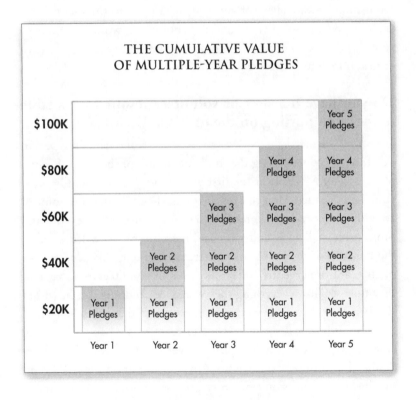

This financial reality is often a sobering fact for groups considering putting on their first Ask Event. Furthermore, if you are not planning to attend our workshop and will be implementing the model on your own, you should definitely not expect to achieve these results. Having said that, in Chapter 7, we will look at ways to increase the bottom-line at your first Ask Event and beyond.

Since nearly every group reports that the Ask Event "was worth so much more than the money," it is important to consider what other outcomes you would like to achieve with the event. Bringing in new donors is a big benefit. In fact, in our tracking of results, we find that 60-70% of the money raised at the first Ask Event comes from new donors.

Whether or not they give at all, every guest will be impressed with the professionalism of your organization and the event. They should leave the Ask Event educated about your work and ready to spread the word to others. This broader community recognition is a critical outcome of the event.

Do you have the staff or volunteer resources available to focus on putting on the first Ask Event?

You will need the equivalent of at least one half-time person dedicated to coordinating the implementation of the entire Raising More Money Model over the first year. This person should become your Team Leader. After that, as the model begins to pay off, some of your other more labor-intensive, less mission-focused events and projects may fall away and more and more time can be dedicated to the cultivation of the donors generated through this process. We often hear from executive directors or senior volunteers who say that they now see how everything they were already doing can fit within this system so that their work feels more focused and productive.

In addition, do you have a full team of six people who will commit to working on this project over the next year? If you are doubtful or unsure, you may want to wait to put on the Ask Event. Just by starting the Point of Entry process, you may uncover many other people who would like to be part of your team.

Is there any other major resistance within the organization to trying this new type of event?

Resistance is natural. The Free One-Hour Ask Event is unlike any other event your organization has done, and people will tend to either confuse it with another event or not understand it at all.

It is well worth talking with these people and addressing their concerns head-on. If there is someone else in your community who has put on a successful Ask Event, ask if they would speak to your board or the individuals who may be questioning the process. Also, I highly recommend showing your board or team the Raising More Money introductory video or DVD, which explains the entire model (in forty-seven minutes) and puts the Ask Event in its proper context. Chapter 5 goes into more depth on how to deal with internal resistance to this event.

REASONS TO WAIT

Even after addressing the above questions, many groups that have been following the Raising More Money Model diligently still get nervous when it comes time to commit to putting on the Free One-Hour Ask Event. It frequently seems that waiting until next year would be a good idea. Sometimes, actually, it is.

The most acceptable reason for waiting is that you have another event scheduled this year, and it would confuse people if you were to put on two events near the same time. It would also overwhelm your staff with double work.

Another reason we often hear is that organizations want to have more Point of Entry Events first. If yours is a brand-new organization with few donors, that may be a valid reason for waiting. Generally, six to nine months of successful Point of Entry Events should give you enough passionate people to serve as Table Captains and guests. The Ask Event itself will generate more interest and more Point of Entry hosts and guests; it actually accelerates the process.

A third possible reason for holding off on doing the event this year is because of staff changes. Some are more significant than others, such as a change in the executive director, the retirement of a beloved leader, or changes in development staff. But sometimes these are the very reasons *not* to postpone the event. A change in leadership—as in the retirement of a Visionary Leader—is often something to be celebrated at the Ask Event. The event serves to remind donors who have been personally loyal to the outgoing leader about the true mission of the organization. We often encourage the outgoing leader to speak at the event about the vision they are passing on and to invite people to continue to support that mission, not just the person who was at the helm.

Ultimately, the unspoken reason most groups want to wait to put on the event is fear. They know that this event is different, they may be concerned about trying to explain the event to board and volunteers, and they may be nervous themselves about putting on a successful event. It feels like too much pressure. They fear the unknown.

If fear is your only true barrier, I encourage you to take the plunge. If you have put together a solid team of four to six people who have helped to put on regular Point of Entry Events, you have enough of a team to undertake the Ask Event. Follow the formulas we suggest for numbers of guests, numbers of Table Captains, and the other ratios listed in our books; choose the date for your event; select your venue; book the room; and don't look back.

The time never looks right for doing something new and different. There will always be good reasons to procrastinate. Probably the main reason for proceeding now is because *you're* there. It takes one person to be the cheerleader for the team. If you are the one who is seriously interested in leaving a legacy of a system that generates lifelong donors, I recommend that you jump in and do it now.

You don't need to start with a large event. Starting with a 100-person event lets you work out the kinks before you roll it out full-scale at your second event—with confidence.

As with most new challenges, at the outset, the risks loom larger than the rewards. Only after you have put on the event, heard the terrific feedback, and tallied up the money raised will you know the rewards. While you will no doubt see many things you wish you had done differently, you will also see the change as donors make multiple-year pledges for unrestricted giving to the mission of your organization. Board members, staff, and volunteers will thank you for reminding them why they got involved in the first place. And don't be surprised when they ask, as the event ends, "Why didn't we do this sooner?"

CHAPTER 4

THE TOP TEN REASONS TO HAVE AN ASK EVENT

Here are the top ten benefits of the Free One-Hour Ask Event, as reported consistently by our workshop alumni, who have been trained and coached through the process to successfully implement the entire model.

BENEFITS OF THE ASK EVENT

1. **It gives people who have been through the first steps of the Raising More Money Model an opportunity to fund the sustaining operations of the organization.**

   After you have educated and inspired people at a Point of Entry, followed up with them to see if and how they might like to become involved, and then had many personal contacts with them along the Cultivation Superhighway, there will come a time when the fruit has naturally ripened and is ready to be picked. The Free One-Hour Ask Event is that opportunity. And because the cultivation process has shown these people that they can trust you to use their gifts wisely and put the money where it will be used best, many of these donors will be willing to make unrestricted gifts toward your operational needs for many years to come.

2.   It gives new people who might not come to a Point of Entry an opportunity to be exposed to your work.

The Table Captains at the Free One-Hour Ask Event often have access to people you would love to have attend a Point of Entry. While Table Captains are certainly encouraged to bring each of their guests to a Point of Entry, many guests will decline such an invitation and prefer to just come and sit at the table of a friend at the Ask Event. The powerful program at the Ask Event, combined with the energy of the crowd in the room, makes for a dramatic introduction to the organization. For these guests, the Ask Event serves as their Point of Entry; it piques their curiosity enough so that they want to learn more.

3.   It is consistent with the new reality we live in.

The Free One-Hour Ask Event honors people's busy schedules by keeping to a sixty-minute schedule. It is straightforward and permission-based. It tells the organization's story in a thoughtful manner and does not pressure or strong-arm anyone to give. It lets people choose for themselves if and how they want to become involved.

4.   It gives people the opportunity to declare their ongoing support for your work by becoming a member of your Multiple-Year Giving Society.

Although they know they can give to you one year at a time, a certain percentage of these donors will be happy to make a pledge to give substantial amounts for at least five years in a row. They will understand what you are trying to accomplish and be proud to publicly declare their support by becoming a founding member of this giving society.

5. **Your organization can cultivate these loyal donors in special ways so they can become more involved, introduce others, and continue to give at increasing levels.**

    The biggest benefit of the Multiple-Year Giving Society is that it allows people to clearly identify themselves as being "with you" on the mission. They are asking to be part of your organization's family. They are asking to be kept informed and involved. This allows you to meet with them individually and in groups for special cultivation activities and to share with them the plans for the next phase of fulfilling your mission, including capital campaigns, endowment, and restricted major gifts.

6. **It gives your loyal supporters a once-a-year opportunity to reconnect with what they love about your organization; it is a natural "feel-good" event.**

    The Ask Event becomes a special reunion for insiders who may choose to be Table Captains year after year. For many, this is their one active form of involvement with the organization, and it gives them great pleasure to invite people to learn more about the organization. Since they understand how the event works, they are not afraid that their friends will feel pressured to give, and they look forward to the event each year.

7. **It reconnects your board, staff, and volunteers to their passion for your mission.**

    When they attend the event and look around the room at the crowd that has assembled to hear about your work, and when they listen to the impressive and inspiring program, everyone involved with your organization will be very proud. We often hear stories of board members who say, "Why didn't we do this sooner? This is great; this is why I got involved here in the first place."

8. **If you repeat the event annually, you will be able to phase out—over time—many of the other more labor-intensive events your organization puts on.**

Eventually, as the bottom-line increases and more and more people come to trust the power of the Ask Event, volunteers and board members will begin to question the need for some of the other events. You will be able to assign a specific purpose to each event within your system, and some will naturally fall away.

9. **It focuses all of your Point of Entry efforts towards a goal.**

Once you get into an annual cycle with Ask Events, all of your Point of Entry Events and follow-up efforts become opportunities to introduce new people and develop relationships with potential Table Captains and guests.

10. **It is likely to raise more money in one hour than any other event.**

Nothing speaks louder than results, and these will be noticed quickly. Furthermore, people often comment about how much easier and less expensive this event is to put on than other, more "entertainment-oriented" events.

CHAPTER 5

OVERCOMING INTERNAL
RESISTANCE TO THE ASK EVENT

One of the most challenging barriers to proceeding toward the Ask Event is internal resistance from your staff or board. People resist change; it's natural. Therefore, if you are permanently shifting your organization's fundraising from the old-reality approach of strong-arming and scarcity to a new-reality, abundance-based approach, resistance is to be expected.

Before you become too absorbed in feeling sorry for yourself and complaining, recall that you have undertaken something major. You are a change agent, a whistle-blower who calls attention to the old way to mark the end of that era. Twenty years from now, when you come back and see your organization thriving and funding its annual operating "shortfall" from the interest of its substantial endowment, all of the resistance you are encountering right now will seem insignificant. You will see that the work you are doing now is what set your organization on a new course.

That said, it still doesn't feel good to have people you work with and care about, people you respect for their deep commitment to your shared mission, tell you openly or otherwise that they think your plan won't work, or that they are concerned that the Ask Event will feel "tacky" and cheap, or that they wouldn't want to invite anyone to come to it until they see it firsthand.

Here is some simple advice about overcoming resistance from your board, staff, and volunteers, and a strategy for gradually gaining the buy-in you will need to sustain the model.

Give up on trying to win everyone over to this method. It may take several years to accomplish that. You do not need everyone's buy-in to begin. (After all, if they were to tell the truth, not everyone loves the golf tournament or the gala!)

Make a list of the people whose approval you absolutely must have to go forward. This should include the executive director and at least one influential person on your board. Ideally, you would also have the buy-in of a few of your top volunteers, including one or more who have been leaders in some of your other fundraising events. Finally, be sure this list includes some of your long-time donors and supporters. Their approval for this new approach will be helpful to win over the others.

Meet with each of these people and get them excited about the model. Show them the Raising More Money introductory video or DVD or have them visit our Web site to view the brief online pre-recorded presentation of the model. You can even sit with them as they watch it. Share with them your commitment to try out the model in the organization. Let them ask questions. Tell them what you are trying to accomplish.

Don't be surprised if they say yes right away. After all, they are as committed to the future sustainability of the organization as you are. They may only have been attached to the old fundraising process for lack of a better model. You may find an early adopter in the bunch who will help you enlist the support of others.

Eventually, get enough support to convene a meeting to let people air their concerns. Have your champions in attendance to speak on behalf of the new plan.

Get enough support to at least "try" the model for one year, using a few supporters as your team members. If you can work the model on a small scale, towards a small first-year Ask Event, the results will speak for themselves.

Invite those who are less convinced to attend a Point of Entry Event, even if they already know all about the work of the organization. They are the perfect people to critique your Point of Entry Events and give you feedback about how to improve them.

Invite these same "skeptics" to attend your first Ask Event as VIPs and sit at a table hosted by another board member or top volunteer whom they know and would feel comfortable with. "Bless and release" those who truly do not wish to attend.

Let the process work its magic. Treat these people as you would any other important Ask Event guests. Let them become absorbed in the powerful and engaging one-hour program you have put together. No doubt, this event will turn some of these skeptics into your biggest donors and champions.

Graciously thank these people for attending the event and include everyone (even the people you "blessed and released") next year in whatever way they would like to be included.

By following this simple, permission-based approach to honoring your insiders and letting them buy into the process at whatever level they are comfortable, you will slowly win over many initial naysayers to the model. In the process, the scales will tip due to the many new people in the community becoming involved with your organization. And these people, who have been connected naturally to the work of the organization, will have resources of their own to contribute.

CHAPTER 6

LEVERAGING THE ASK

Looking ahead to putting on the Ask Event, there are several components of the model necessary to leverage each Ask, all revolving around your newly-established Multiple-Year Giving Society. Let's first look at these broader tools for making the most of each Ask before we discuss ways to increase the bottom-line.

MULTIPLE-YEAR GIVING SOCIETY

The Multiple-Year Giving Society is an essential component of the Raising More Money Model. It is not optional. Without it, you will have a strong base of one-year-at-a-time donors. With it, you have a key element of your self-generating system. This Multiple-Year Giving Society becomes the new, higher order of giving for those who truly support your cause. Giving at one of these levels is the donor's way of saying, "Count me in. I really do understand what your organization is up to. You have my permission to come back to me, to keep me involved, and to ask me for more." From the perspective of the organization, members of your Multiple-Year Giving Society become a distinct group to cultivate and involve.

Launching your Multiple-Year Giving Society in no way precludes single-year giving. If you have a strong base of year-to-year donors, you will of course want to invite them to become part of your new, multiple-year program. If they decline this invitation, their names will still be listed in your annual report using the same categories you have used in the past (for a sample annual report, see page 48).

Once you have established your Multiple-Year Giving Society, you will want to list its members prominently as a separate category in your annual report, right above your annual givers. Be sure to use a big headline that calls attention to the fact that these people have agreed to give at these levels for the number of years stated.

Organizations are often reluctant to launch a Multiple-Year Giving Society. They usually say something like: "Our donors would never go for that." In truth, they are usually looking at it from their perspective, which is to say they would feel uncomfortable asking for multiple-year pledges.

Remember, the multiple-year Ask is not for the organization; the multiple-year Ask is for the donor. Multiple-Year Donors are people who *already* love you and in many cases have been giving to you, year after year, with relatively little contact or cultivation. Now you are giving them an opportunity to come forward and declare themselves part of your organization's family. Some will say, "No, thank you." Others will ask: "What took you so long to notice?"

In this fundraising model, entrance into your Multiple-Year Giving Society requires a minimum of a five-year pledge of $1,000 per year. Those organizations bold enough to write those few extra words "for five years" on their pledge cards almost always wish they had done it sooner, especially since the pledge payoff rate is greater than 95%. Sometimes reticent groups back off of this rule and ask for a three-year pledge. Invariably they come back to report that after seeing how many people selected that multiple-year option, they wish they had increased it to five years or more. Five years goes by pretty quickly in the life of a donor, three years even more so. For many established organizations, I recommend starting with a ten-year commitment.

Without the multiple-year Ask, you are back to a standard old-reality, annual gifts program which, if done well, leaves the donor quietly giving year after year. Multiple-year asking, if done consistently, following the interim cultivation steps between each Ask, will grow your base exponentially and build the lifelong donors you are looking for.

UNITS OF SERVICE

Your Units of Service are the giving levels within your Multiple-Year Giving Society. They are the various bite-sized amounts of unrestricted funding you will be asking for. Your Multiple-Year Giving Society should have a total of only three levels. There are two options for these levels:

Option One:
- $ 1,000/year x five years
- $ 5,000/year x five years
- $10,000/year x five years

Option Two:
- $ 1,000/year x five years
- $10,000/year x five years
- $25,000/year x five years

Your answer to the following question will determine which of these options to use:

What is the single largest gift made by an individual to your organization in the past two years? It may take a bit of research to find the answer to that question, or you might know it right away. If the single largest gift from an individual is *less than $10,000*, you should choose Option One. If the single largest gift from an individual is *$10,000 or more*, you should choose Option Two.

In either case, there are two more boxes on the pledge card, followed by additional payment information:

- I would like to give $_____ for _____ years.
- Please contact me. I have other thoughts to share.

DESIGNING YOUR UNITS OF SERVICE

The main thing to keep in mind as you design your Units of Service is that you will be making it clear to your donors that these levels represent arbitrary chunks of needed, unrestricted operating funds. They will be giving at these levels because they believe in your overall mission. They trust you to get the job done. If they have questions about your use of funds, they can review your audit.

For this reason, your units or levels do not have to be accurate to the penny. The easiest way to justify your Units of Service is to take your total budget or total budget shortfall and divide it by roughly the number of people you serve in a year. For example, let's assume the total budget for your organization is $2 million. After deducting your public funding and the fees you charge your art patrons or health-care patients, you arrive at a number of $200,000 you must raise privately each year. Since you are aiming for your lowest unit to be $1,000, what variable could you divide $200,000 by to arrive at $1,000? In other words, what do you serve or provide 200 of each year? Families, homeless women, acres of land being preserved, pregnant teenagers, or dance patrons? That will give you your lowest unit. Then work up from there based on the variable you have chosen. It all needs to hang together and make logical sense to a donor.

Once you have designed your units, do not change them. On the contrary, try to universalize them within your system. Include these units in all your in-person solicitations. The pledge card you design for your Multiple-Year Giving Society will be the same pledge card you use in all of your face-to-face solicitations, including the Free One-Hour Ask Event. A sample pledge card can be found on page 123.

As you become comfortable with the levels you have designed, you will find it easy to make all of your Asks, including your one-on-one Asks, at one of these levels. I often tell the story from the school where the model was developed about asking for a contribution from the owner of a large, privately-held corporation. This man had attended a Point of Entry Event, had been well followed-up with and cultivated. He was definitely ready to be asked. Because of his heavy travel schedule, I had been unable to connect with him by phone to even schedule a time we could get together to discuss his gift.

A month or so later, I happened to nearly bump into this man as he was coming out of an elevator in the lobby of an office building. Our twenty-second conversation went something like this:

"Hi, Terry, how are you? I know I owe you a call."

"Yes, that's OK. You know why I was calling."

"Yep, I do. What's everybody giving?"

"$25,000 a year for five years to 'Sponsor a Classroom' of kids."

"That sounds great. Sign us up!"

If you have followed the model, not skipped over any of the steps, and have your Units of Service well thought out, an Ask can be that simple. So it is well worth taking the time to custom design the Units of Service that best suit your organization. In the case of this man, after each Ask, he attended more of our high-end donor Free Feel-Good Cultivation Events. With close personal follow up over time, he has become a major donor to the organization's capital and endowment campaigns, while continuing to give a $25,000 gift annually as part of his pledge to the Multiple-Year Giving Society.

NAMING YOUR LEVELS AND GIVING SOCIETY

Your Units of Service or multiple-year giving levels should have names that relate to your programs or services. Your units also must relate logically to one another. This can be accomplished easily if you use the same variable in naming them. As with everything else in our model, they must personalize your work. For example, if your lowest level was to sponsor a child, your middle level could be to sponsor a family, and your highest level could be to sponsor a neighborhood or a community. A sports group might choose as its units: sponsor a player, a team, and a league.

If you do not have obvious categories, consider more generic names like friend, mentor, or advocate. For advocacy or social change groups, we have used levels such as $1,000 to mobilize five advocates who each train 200 families a year. The name of the category must be brief. Using this same example, the official name of the unit would be "mobilize five advocates." Then, next to it in smaller type, could be a statement such as "each advocate trains 200 families a year."

Take some time to come up with a strong overall name for your Multiple-Year Giving Society, since it will be with your organization for years. Consider the name of a prominent person who has been a champion for your cause. Or perhaps the name of one of your founders or founding board members. It is also fine to use a more generic title, like the traditional Founder's Society, Legacy Club, or the Friends of (your organization).

CHALLENGE GIFTS

One final leveraging tool which can make a major difference in your asking success is the Challenge Gift. This is an ideal enhancement if you have major donors who are ready to give in advance of your Ask Event. Whether given by one donor or pooled by several donors into a Challenge Gift Fund, when used as a matching gift, it gives the donor the perception of a bargain. And we all love a bargain. Here is how it works.

First, go through your donor lists and rank your donors by giving potential. Then rank them again based on their passion for your cause. The handful who shake out at the top of both lists are your candidates for giving funds that can be used as part of the Challenge Gift.

Next, set your goal. Say you want to raise $100,000. Ask the top five donors from your lists if they would each consider giving you $10,000. Tell them you would like to use their collective $50,000 as a one-to-one match for gifts from other donors.

Then, at the usual time of year for your annual campaign, go to your other potential donors, the ones who are a bit farther down the lists. Tell them this year you have been presented with a wonderful opportunity: a group of your major donors has come together to stimulate the campaign to reach a new level. They have put $50,000 into a Challenge Gift Fund. Every dollar given will be matched one-to-one by this Challenge Fund. And there is a deadline by when you must fulfill the challenge.

For donors who work for a company that matches employee contributions, this can mean a four-to-one leverage of their gift. They give $1,000, their company matches it so it becomes $2,000, and your Challenge Gift Fund donors match that amount, so the total gift becomes $4,000. The value of leveraging their gift in this way will not be lost on most of these folks.

Be sure to clarify with your Challenge Fund donors—the ones who seed the initial $50,000 in this example—what kind of a challenge they want to offer. Will their money match other donations dollar-for-dollar, two-for-one or three-for-one? Also decide in advance how you want to handle donor pledges. Will they "count" in the match? Will those who pledge still give you the full amount of the Challenge Gift even if you don't fulfill the match? Will the employer's matching portion of each gift count in the base gift to be matched by your Challenge Gift Fund?

Another highly effective twist: Use the Challenge Gift Fund to match only the increased portion of a donor's gift. In other words, if they gave $500 last year, the Challenge Fund will match whatever amount the donor gives beyond $500 this year.

Think through all the ways you can promote the Challenge Gift Fund. Decide if you want to showcase the founding donor or donors to the fund. How can they help you bring in more donors? Can you write about it in your newsletter, include it in other mailings, send out a special announcement about it, kick it off at the annual event?

Before you announce the Challenge Fund, put together several foolproof strategies for fulfilling on it. You will need ten gifts of $5,000, twenty gifts of $1,000, etc. Be sure that you, personally, are excited about the potential of the Challenge Fund for your organization. What will it provide in the way of programs and services? Can you articulate this to potential donors?

People want to know that you need their support and that you will use it wisely. The more you can leverage their gift, and the more of a "bargain" they feel they are getting for it, the better.

RECOGNIZING THE MULTI-YEAR PLEDGE IN YOUR ANNUAL REPORT

Let's look at how all of this would be displayed on your annual report.

SAMPLE ANNUAL REPORT
NEIGHBORS IN NEED SOCIETY

Our thanks to these generous donors who have pledged this level of support for the next five years:

Sponsor a Neighborhood
$25,000

Sponsor a Family
$10,000

Sponsor a Child
$1,000

_____
_____
_____
_____
_____

ANNUAL FUND DONORS

$25,000+

$1,000 - $4,999

$10,000 - $24,999

$500 - $999

$5,000 - $9,999

$100 - $499

If your organization currently publishes an annual report, it is probably similar in format to the bottom half of this sample. It lists your donors segmented by the size of their gifts.

Once you launch your Multiple-Year Giving Society, list those Multiple-Year Donors separately on the top part of the report. Name the society and each giving level and make it clear that these donors have pledged to give at this level each year for five years.

One more option, if you have fewer than five donors in your Multiple-Year Giving Society after your first Ask Event, is to use the bottom half of the form only, with an asterisk to denote those members of the society and a note near the top or bottom to clarify that the asterisk denotes a five year pledge at this level. Some people will wonder how to get an asterisk next to their name next year!

As always, be sure to have all your donors tell you if and how they would like their name(s) to be listed.

Using these tools to leverage each Ask will give you the framework to increase the bottom-line, the subject of our next chapter.

CHAPTER 7

FIVE WAYS TO INCREASE
THE BOTTOM-LINE

There are five ways to increase the results of your Ask Event and ensure that you meet or exceed the predictable results.

SPONSOR

Have the event sponsored by a corporation or foundation that already knows you and supports your work. You can determine the dollar amount of the sponsorship. At a minimum, it should cover the costs of putting on the event.

As your event grows in size and stature each year, you may be able to raise the price of the sponsorship and offer more visibility for the corporation than they would have received for sponsoring your golf tournament or other smaller special event. One organization we work with has a $250,000 sponsor for their large Ask Event.

Ideally, you will have only one significant sponsor, headed by a person or group of people who have been involved as volunteers or beneficiaries of your work. In addition to making a large sponsorship gift, they may participate in the program, perhaps as a Testimonial Speaker or the Pitch Person.

CHALLENGE GIFT

As discussed earlier, having a significant Challenge Gift can make a big difference in the bottom-line results of your Ask Event.

In addition, it lets you start your event with a boost of confidence. This gift from one or more major donors is announced just prior to the Pitch. Ideally, the Challenge Gift is set up as a true match for some or all of the money raised at the event, giving your guests a sense of urgency and a sense that their gift is being leveraged. They will perceive it as a "bargain" of sorts, to make a gift to you that day.

MORE TABLE CAPTAINS

The most obvious way to increase the bottom-line is to have more people attend your event, which, to follow this model, would require more Table Captains.

The results of your Ask Event correlate directly to the number of people in attendance. In other words, the more guests you have, the more money you will raise.

If you take this to heart, you will allow the lead time necessary to go through the preliminary steps to generate a long list of Table Captains.

Specifically, this will require two things: putting on regularly-scheduled, well attended Point of Entry Events, and making a detailed Treasure Map with your team of the network of people in your organization's universe.

Until your Point of Entry Events have become part of everyday life at your organization, you will not have the model solidly entrenched. You should be so comfortable with the content and format and venue for your Point of Entry that you could put on this sizzling one-hour introductory event on a moment's notice. The more Point of Entry guests you have, the more passionate Table Captains you will have.

The Treasure Map is your most powerful tool for identifying groups of potential Table Captains that are right under your nose, yet you may never have thought of them. Rather than relying on the same old prospects, most notably by pressuring your board members to once again "hit up" their friends, you should branch out to all the other individuals and groups that are already demonstrating their support by being involved in some way in the day-to-day life of your organization. Detailed instructions for creating a Treasure Map are included in the Appendix, page 215.

Your Treasure Map will change rapidly as you implement the model, so I recommend you make a new Treasure Map at least twice a year. Many groups do this quarterly.

HIGHER PERCENTAGE OF "RIPENED FRUIT"

By now, you have probably had the thought: "Why is only 20% ripened fruit required at an Ask Event? Why not more than that?" You can see that the bottom-line results also correlate with the percentage of people who attended a true Point of Entry, received a Follow-Up Call, and were properly cultivated following our permission-based system, so you know they are ready to give.

Clearly, the more "ripened fruit" at the Ask Event, the better. Groups that have 80-90% of their guests in this category raise several times more money than those with only 20%.

After the first Ask Event, every single group comes to this realization on their own and suddenly becomes more interested in the rest of the model. They recognize that for the same amount of work it takes to put on an Ask Event, they could multiply their net results if they just took the time up front to more fully cultivate their donors.

The sad fact is that most nonprofits are so locked into the treadmill of survival-based fundraising, that the thought of planting the seeds, tilling the soil, and waiting until the time is right for the harvest, is unrealistic for the first Ask Event. If we could *make* you do that, we would. Instead, we have the 20% ripened-fruit minimum rule.

MORE ASK EVENTS PER YEAR

I hesitate to suggest this option, but many groups use it with great success—putting on more than one Ask Event per year. While your first event may raise more money than any other fundraising event in your organization's history, if you have followed the model, this amount will include all of your five-year pledges. In other words, the actual amount of cash (or credit card or stock) gifts you will have at the end of the first year's event will be a little more than one-fifth of the total. And that amount may not be enough to cover the operating shortfall you have for the first year. Thus, the first reason for putting on more than one Ask Event per year is to raise more money.

And for groups whose first event is in the spring, a second event in November can help to get them onto an annual cycle of a November event, which is the single best month to hold the event (unless you are in a resort community where you have seasonal visitors—in which case April is best).

The second and best reason for holding multiple Ask Events per year is location. We work with one organization in a mid-sized market that puts on twelve Ask Events per year. They have segmented their area with great care to know how far people will drive to go to such an event and where people draw the invisible boundary lines between communities. They have had great success.

Another example is a group with a large geographic "catchment area," such as part of a state, an entire state, a region, or the entire country.

If you are considering multiple events, put on your first event in your main market first. Ideally, this will be the area closest to *you*. This will allow you to test out all the variables in a community you are familiar with before you take the event "on the road."

There is one other reason for multiple events that may occasionally have some legitimacy; namely, the size of your venue. We worked with a well-known and well-supported fundraising foundation for an historic landmark building. They insisted on having their Ask Event in the building, but it could only accommodate 100 people. In spite of our advice that they hold the event in a larger venue to save themselves having to put on multiple events, they insisted. They held four Ask Events their first year, each in their gorgeous building. Because they had been meticulous in putting on their Point of Entry Events, doing their follow-up and cultivation according to the model, they "batched" their guests into four separate groups, based on which people were ready to be asked to give. Needless to say, they did fabulously.

However, by the second year, they realized that putting on four Ask Events using the same team of volunteers and staff in the same community was a bit taxing. They now put on one large Ask Event each year, at a downtown hotel. With such a high percentage of ripened fruit—people who have already seen their landmark building at the Point of Entry Events and were then further cultivated—they no longer feel the need to hold four smaller Ask Events per year there.

Focusing on these five leverage points will give you more control in predicting your results. Let's turn next to your plan for tracking those results.

CHAPTER 8

KEEPING TRACK OF YOUR RESULTS

We tell people every day, "If you are serious about leaving the legacy of a self-sustaining individual giving program for your organization, it will need to include a data tracking system easy enough for everyone to use." Heads nod, people agree—in theory. Yet in day-to-day practice, people ask, "What kind of tracking system do we need and what, exactly, should we be tracking?"

YOUR TRACKING SYSTEM

After many years of offering our workshops to groups of all sizes and all levels of sophistication, we have found that there are four essential criteria for a good data tracking system if you are using the Raising More Money Model.

First, it needs to track relationships and contacts over time, not just people's basic contact information (name, address, phone number) and gift history.

Second, it needs to be easy to use—by everyone on your team. It is no longer sufficient to relegate data entry to a clerical person who often has no relationship to the donor cultivation process. In this model, every member of your team needs to feel comfortable entering notes into the system—notes about every single contact they have with a donor. This is because, over time, many people in your organization will naturally have contact with each donor, depending on the donor's interests and involvement. You want a record of each of those contacts to live on in one central database.

Many of our groups have active volunteers with well-equipped home offices and Internet access. Giving these high-level, dedicated volunteers access to a Web-based tracking system and permission to enter their own notes lets them feel that much more connected to the fundraising process and to the organization. These systems can be set up with special password access to what is, in effect, a private Web site storing all your data.

Over time, as the volunteers and staff move on, these notes live in this permanent repository, owned by the organization.

The only exception to this process of entering information is the financial data. This needs to be entered by one or two well-trained people who understand how to account for outright gifts versus pledges, all of which your system should allow you to do with ease, ideally while tied into your organization's main accounting system. In addition, you will need to decide who has access to viewing this financial data.

Third, the application should interface well with your Web site. This will allow the information from forms, surveys, event registrations, and e-commerce (donations especially) to be captured directly in the database.

Fourth, for the system to be an effective communication tool for follow-up, it should be able to deliver and store both individual and mass e-mail. It should integrate with your calendar and tickler system as well.

There are many good tracking systems, including Web-based systems as well as more traditional desktop software systems. If you already have a system you are happy with, stay with it, so long as it is easy enough for everyone on your team to use for tracking all donor cultivation. To ensure that there is a product that is completely integrated to the Raising More Money Model, we have developed Raising More Money Next Step.

No matter which tracking system you decide to use, today's technology makes it possible to accumulate critical knowledge more easily and less expensively than ever before. Over time, you will see more ways to customize your data tracking system to the model, extrapolating reports and charts to summarize your progress. While it may seem like a daunting task, launching a centralized tracking system is an invaluable and lasting legacy you will be leaving for your organization.

WHAT TO TRACK

As you consider what to track, a good place to begin is to look at what you are already tracking. You may be surprised by how much (or how little) data you may already have. Do you have lists of current donors and volunteers, lists of board members, past board members, staff, and former staff? What other information do you collect on these people? Do you track which events they may have attended, which mailings they may have responded to, who invited them to their first Point of Entry? Ultimately, even if you adopt a new data system, it will be important to know what information you already possess.

If you presume that every person who attends your Point of Entry may become a lifelong donor, you need to begin tracking key information from the point of initial contact. The basic contact information card that each person fills out (your Capture the Names tool) can become your primary source. This should include their name, address, phone, e-mail address, and the name of the person who referred them to your organization. As this information is entered into your database, you will begin a log of your contacts with this person, entering the date of the Point of Entry Event they attended and the relationship of the referring contact when one exists.

Next, track your Follow-Up Call. Note the date you called, any messages left before you reached them, and what they said on the call. If possible, have the five-step Follow-Up Call as a form in your database and enter each guest's answers to those questions. When you ask the fifth question, "Is there anyone else you can think of who we ought to invite to attend our _____ (Point of Entry)?" and they suggest others, right then is the time to begin a separate record for these new people as well. A good database/contact management system should enable you to track the relationships between people in your system, which is a very valuable cross-referencing tool. Make sure that your note for each contact (such as the Follow-Up Call) includes a date for your next contact and that this links to an action item in your daily planner for that future date.

This same tracking process holds true throughout the Cultivation Superhighway. Each contact—whether by phone or in-person—must be tracked with notes and next actions, all tied to dates and, ultimately, to someone's daily "to-do" calendar. The difference between successful and lackluster cultivation is related to the amount of listening and note keeping you do in your dialog with donors.

TRACKING THE FREE ONE-HOUR ASK EVENT

What should you track related to the Free One-Hour Ask Event? You will want to track data on each individual guest, as well as collective data from the overall event.

Data on each individual guest includes: did the person RSVP, did the person attend, the name of the person's Table Captain, the amount of the donor's gift or pledge on the day of the event, and the dates these pledges were paid off or increased (perhaps at subsequent events).

Data on the overall event includes the names of everyone who accepted the invitation, the total number of guests who attended your Ask Event, total gifts received from all donors (including pledges) on the day of the event, and total gifts and pledges received in the next three months from Ask Event guests.

After the Ask Event, you will want to track the entire follow-up process. As you call each new donor, what are they saying? Who would they like to invite to a Point of Entry? Would they like to host a Point of Entry? Would they like to be a Table Captain again next year? Did any of their guests express interest in becoming Table Captains? What about the people who left their table without turning in a completed pledge card? What, if anything, did they say as they left? Be sure to note these comments in the file for that guest, including any next steps needed.

BEYOND THE ASK EVENT

For future Ask Events, you can collect data on donors who become Table Captains, donors who pay off or increase their gift at the next Ask Event, the number of repeat attendees, etc.

As for the thank-you and recognition process, you need to track when and how each donor was thanked. What other feedback have they given you since the event? What is the next contact or next step with each of these donors? Is that next step tied to the "to-do" calendar for that date?

What about Free Feel-Good Cultivation Events? You can use your tracking system to note in each donor's record that they were invited, whether or not they accepted, and, ultimately, whether they attended.

In other words, your tracking system should be the one solid, reliable repository for the chronology of every single contact with that donor. Everyone who has access to your database will come to count on this as the sole source for up-to-the-minute information on each donor, potential donor, and volunteer.

More importantly, the tracking system will then allow you to make queries of the data in the system and to make reports of any information you need. Who attended which event? Who were the major donors at your Ask Event? Who are the people who need a Follow-Up Call, a visit from a board member, or a thank-you note? No matter how good a system is at collecting information, it must also allow for easy retrieval of the information you need.

GETTING READY

CHAPTER 9

FIRST STEPS

I t's official! You've decided to put on the Free One-Hour Ask
Event within the next year. To mitigate your excitement and fear,
and to make the process more real for everyone concerned, there are
a number of specific next steps to be taken.

ASSEMBLING YOUR TEAM

Now is the time to get serious about who is on the team. Do
not draft people into service just because they are on your board or
your development committee. Take the time to talk with them one-
on-one, show them the Raising More Money video or DVD, and get
their full buy-in to the process.

This fundraising system is a significant commitment that requires
people who *want* to be part of the process. It is better to start with a
small but hard-working, passionate team (four is the minimum size)
than to have a larger team of people who are not fully committed.
Those more peripheral people will make ideal Table Captains, but
won't be strong core team members.

The ideal team has a mixture of staff, board, and volunteers. It
should not be heavily weighted in any area. Each person needs to
commit to be part of the team for at least the next year. They should
each have read *Raising More Money—A Step-by-Step Guide to Building Lifelong Donors,* which goes into greater depth about each step of
the model. If you are fortunate enough to know another group in

your community using this model, it would be ideal if your team members could attend one of their Point of Entry Events as well as their Ask Event to witness the process firsthand.

Assemble the team for the first planning meeting and cover each of the following aspects of the Ask Event.

CHOOSING THE BEST DATE

Choosing the date right now is essential. Not just the month or the week you plan to have the event, but the exact date. Then choose where to have it, and reserve that venue now.

Let's look at the factors that will help you decide when to have the Ask Event. Having tested out every month of the year, we have found the best months to have the Ask Event are May or November. May is after the spring thaw, before school lets out, and long enough after the year-end holidays for the Table Captains to fill their tables. Also by May, the seasonal "snow-bird" residents have returned to their primary residence and are ready to attend your event. November (and even early December) are also ideal because they are near the end of the year and the holiday season, which is the time when most individuals make their largest charitable gifts.

The only exception we have made to this part of the formula is for communities with many seasonal residents. If your organization is located in such a community, you will want to plan your event for a month when those seasonal residents are in your community. Because of the lead time to plan the Ask Event, recruit Table Captains, put on the requisite number of Point of Entry Events, and make the necessary Follow-Up Calls, April is often the best month for these "snow-bird" communities.

The biggest barrier most groups encounter in choosing a date is the number of their own existing activities. Be it the graduation ceremony, the spring arts festival, or the grant writing deadline, squeezing in one more event is more than most good development staff can bear to consider.

Chapter 2 gave you the basic template for the Four Kinds of Events we recognize in the Raising More Money Model. Just understanding how each of your existing events can be easily transformed into one of these mission-centered events will help you to integrate your disparate efforts. Furthermore, it will help you identify those events you are now doing which may be eliminated over time, once you have won everyone over to the Ask Event. Even then, you will want to have at least one Point of Entry Event per month plus two Free Feel-Good Cultivation Events per year.

You should be designing an annual schedule of events—what we call a System of Events—that can become part of the legacy you leave for your organization (see page 23). While it may take two to three years to rotate the months of your existing events so that your Ask Event can be in May or November, your Free Feel-Goods in the next season, and your Point of Entry Events monthly, it is well worth thinking this entire process through now—at the beginning—as you schedule your first Ask Event.

For example, in planning the first Ask Event, many groups find that they already have their big banquet or other fundraising event scheduled for May or November or a month close enough to pose a conflict. Is there enough lead time to move the other event? Or can you plan your first Ask Event for the opposite season and then move it the following year to your 'ideal' month? Many groups we train and coach end up putting on two smaller Ask Events in the first year, in order to position their calendar for a fall Ask Event the following year, without "wasting" a season without an event.

As to best days of the week and best time of day to schedule the first event, we recommend Tuesday, Wednesday, or Thursday for breakfast or lunch. Absolutely do not do this event for dinner or even over the cocktail hour or just for dessert. It needs to be a daytime event. Dinner events come with their own unwritten ground rules—generally a ticket price for admission, plus the expectation of spending additional money on tangible goods or services. If they are asked to give at a dinner event, people tend to give just enough to cover the cost of the dinner. An inexpensive breakfast or lunch is free of the "baggage" associated with dinner events and gives guests the freedom to choose either to give to your mission or not to give at all.

To decide between breakfast or lunch, consider the time that would work best for most of your guests. Working people tend to prefer an early breakfast that they can drive to before they start their work day. Folks who have a little more flexibility to start their day later will prefer lunch. You will never please everyone; aim to please the majority. If you already know the location of the event, this may also influence the time of day that you choose: How accessible is this location to the freeway? Is there good parking? Is it easy to find? Will people be able to get in and out quickly?

BOOKING THE VENUE

After you have decided when to hold the event, you can zero in on your ideal venue. Many groups deliberate over whether or not to have their event at an upscale hotel versus right in their own lunch-room or meeting space. I generally recommend going upscale for the Ask Event. It sends out a message that you are legitimate, profes-sional, and here to stay. Save your office or program venue for your Point of Entry Events. The only exceptions we have made to this are for groups with elegant historical or architectural buildings for which the building itself is related to the organization's mission. If these groups have the space to accommodate a large crowd seated comfort-ably at round tables, it is fine for them to host the Ask Event in their own venue. For everyone else, we recommend a hotel ballroom or nice church hall. In smaller rural communities, we recommend hav-ing the Ask Event in the best wedding venue in town.

Your next concern in booking your venue should be price. To determine that, start with your biggest budget item: food. All the food should be cold and pre-set when the guests arrive. You do not want to have serving people distracting your guests during those precious sixty minutes when you will want their undivided attention. We will talk more about the budget and food later in this chapter. The only other budget item you may have difficulty getting donated is the cost of the audio/visual services on the day of the event. You will need a sound system and the equipment to project your video profession-ally. This can be pricey. We recommend, all told, budgeting $20-25 per person. Note that this does not include the cost of producing your seven-minute video, which we will discuss in Chapter 13.

SETTING YOUR GOALS:
MONEY RAISED AND NUMBER OF GUESTS

When it comes to setting your financial goal for the event, here is how to project the bottom-line. Since we only track the results of the groups who attend our workshops and participate in the coaching that comes with the workshop, I can only cite the results for those groups.

The gross amount raised at the Ask Event is a direct function of the number of people in attendance. For groups that we train and coach through the process, an Ask Event with 200 guests should yield at least $100,000 spread out over the five years that the pledges will come in. A 300-person Ask Event would gross $150,000 (again, this includes the pledges). More of these "formulas" are included in the Appendix, page 225.

If you are planning to implement the model on your own, you will need to reduce these projections by at least 40%. While you may do better than this at your first Ask Event, there are so many questions that will come up along the way, the answers to which will be counterintuitive, that you should plan to make some mistakes along the way and factor that into your bottom-line right from the start.

Since the total number of people in attendance is the starting place for your financial projections, it is worth pausing here to consider how big an event you would like to have. We recommend starting no smaller than 100 people, given the amount of work needed to put on the event and the fixed costs (such as video production). This will allow you to introduce this special type of event to your board, volunteers, and donors. Starting small lets you work out the kinks in the program and format before putting on a larger event. Many organizations put on two Ask Events the first year. Their initial success with a smaller event gives them the confidence and the buy-in to move forward quickly.

As for the largest size event, we have one group in a rural area that has 1,000 people at their Ask Event, and several other groups we have trained have 1200-1400 people at their events. While this size may seem impersonal or even unwieldy, these groups always report that the impact (upon guests, staff, and board members) of having so many people assembled for one hour to learn and talk about the work of this one organization far outweighs those concerns.

EVENT PLANNING

While the financial success of your Ask Event will rest on the work of the Table Captains in filling their tables and the quality of each of your program elements, you also need to put some time into planning the more traditional elements of the event. For the event to come off like clockwork in sixty minutes or less, you need to plan every detail of the day-of-event logistics.

Let's start with the ultimate event planning tool, the budget.

Budgeting for the Event

As much as possible, use your well-honed event planning skills to get things donated. You won't need a lot of "stuff" for the event. There are some printed items, something for centerpieces, and a small gift (like apples or pens) to be passed around during the meal. Ask one company or foundation that supports your work if they will help sponsor the event. Make sure their mission or product is in sync with yours, since they will be the only sponsor and will therefore get a lot of visibility.

If you are successful in getting in-kind donations and an event sponsor or underwriter, this should help you cover your remaining budget items: food and audio/visual equipment. The budget is really quite simple and should be modest.

Without an underwriter or sponsor, many groups just take the cost of the event right out of the event proceeds. For our first Ask Event at the school where the model was developed, we raised nearly $1.5 million (including the pledges) and the event for 850 people cost $14,000.

You will have plenty of benchmarks along the way for projecting your revenue from the event such that you can cut back on the number of meals ordered, size of the room, and other expenses in order to keep your budget in scale with projected revenues.

The typical budget for a 200-person Ask Event is $20-25 per person of true out-of-pocket expenses. This does not include the production cost of a video. It presumes you will have some of the costs donated for centerpieces and printing. It does include fixed costs for audio/visual, which are often high and more easily amortized into a larger event.

Typical budget for a 200-person event at a hotel:

Food @ $16 per person including tax and gratuity	$ 3,200
Room rental	waived
Audio/visual	$ 1,000
Printing	$ 200
Centerpieces, favors, table displays	$ 200
Total	$ 4,600

Party Flair
Naming Your Event

Pick a simple name that is linked to the name of your Multiple-Year Giving Society. If your Multiple-Year Giving Society is called the Sponsor-a-Student Society, you could call your event the Sponsor-a-Student Breakfast. The name of the event will remain the same every year, so be sure it is strong enough to stand the test of time.

Some other examples of names for Ask Events are: Gifts in Faith, Circle of Hope, Every Girl Everywhere, Breath of Hope, A Time to Connect, Seeds for the Future, Children's Voices, Gift of Sight, Take Your Place in History.

Logo

Design a logo for the event that can be used each year as well, something that can be easily adapted to the theme of the event.

Theme and Colors

The theme is different than the name, and the theme changes every year. For example, at the Sponsor-a-Student Breakfast, the theme one year was "back to school." Another year it was "alumni," and another year "parents and families." If possible, adapt your logo to each theme, or find an icon you can use in the printed materials and possibly in other displays, such as the centerpieces. Choose the colors you will use consistently in all your materials.

Printed Materials

The theme, then, helps to determine the graphics on your printed materials for the event so that each element is tied together and looks professional.

Here is a list of the items you will need to have printed for the event:

- Save-the-Date cards
- Event Programs
- Brochure (your standard organizational brochure, one per guest)
- Invitations (not necessary for first event; optional for year two and beyond)

Other items you may make by hand or choose to have printed:

- Table tents (centerpieces made of folder paper) with stories of people served
- Table numbers
- Nametags

Centerpieces and Decorations

The theme also influences the centerpieces and other decorations, which should be very simple. The "back to school" themed event had notebooks and crayons as the centerpieces and displays at the nametag table. People got boxes of crayons as party favors, personally passed out to them by students at the school. The alumni theme had graduation caps, scrolled-up diplomas, and pictures of kids going off to their next school, and the party favor was a scrolled up list of the colleges the alumni were now attending, held together with a tassle from a graduation cap. Generally, the materials for the centerpieces are donated.

Menu and Final Meal Count

People tend to be the most concerned about the food: what to serve, and what it will cost? While the food should be simple and plentiful, it is secondary to the one-hour program. The event is over so quickly that people will barely remember what they ate, but they will remember the inspiring program.

Whether your Ask Event is a breakfast or lunch, the food should be cold and pre-set so that no serving people will be distracting your guests from the program. For breakfast events, serve a cold "heavy" continental breakfast, with fruit and juice, breads, yogurt, granola, etc. For lunch events, a chicken Caesar salad works well, with the bread and dessert pre-set on the tables. Some groups putting on lunch events prefer to serve the dessert after the hour-long event ends, so people can mingle if they choose.

The final meal count—the number of meals you are guaranteeing you will pay for—is usually due two to three days before the event. Most caterers will prepare 10-15% more food than the guarantee number, so we recommend having your official final meal count be 10-15% less than the number of people you expect. Be very pessimistic here. If you have Table Captain lists for 200 people, order no more than 170 meals.

Conversely, you should have the hotel or venue set the tables for the full number of people you are expecting. But have them only pre-set the food for seven out of ten places at each table. Alert the catering department that they may have to move some of the pre-set meals once they see how many people actually sit at each table.

Do not fret about this too much. Although the food is the single biggest budget item of the event, it is not the thing people will remember most. Hotels and restaurants are experts at rustling up more food in a pinch, and if all else fails, alert your staff and volunteers to hold off on eating until they are sure there are enough meals. Rest assured that 99% of the time, there are way more empty seats than overflow tables and, likewise, plenty of extra food, in spite of your reduced final meal count.

Seating Chart

Draw out a floor plan (to scale) of the room. Be sure you have enough room for all the necessary round tables of ten, but not so much space that the room seems cavernous. Determine which Table Captains will be seated in which part of the room. Reserve a round table front and center for the people who will be speaking, including the emcee, the Visionary Leader, the Testimonial Speakers, and the Pitch Person. Generally speaking, your higher-ranking Table Captains (probably your board and other donors) should have tables that are relatively front and center in the room. Tables along the perimeter are less desirable, and tables at the back are the least desirable. That being said, every table in the room should offer an excellent view of the speakers, either directly or via large screen projection.

DAY OF EVENT LOGISTICS

The more you can anticipate every detail of the flow of the event, the more likely it is to go smoothly and according to the plan. Having people trained in what can go wrong and how to think on their feet will save the event coordinator for the bigger decisions or, if you are lucky, for enjoying the event!

Let's take it one step at a time.

Pre-Event

In spite of the best work of your Table Captains to properly prepare their guests, most guests will not know what to expect when they arrive. They will not trust that the event will last only one hour or that they do not really have to give money. While they may be smiling and polite as they walk into the building, underneath those smiles they will be skeptical and a bit suspicious. Therefore, everything you can do to warm them up and get them to trust you before the event begins is a plus. It is worth putting some thought into all of the pre-event elements and even making them a bit theatrical.

Greeters

Have greeters strategically placed outside or near the front doors and again at every place people need to turn or take an escalator or elevator to get to the room where the event is being held. Choose greeters who are truly linked to your work, whose welcoming smile, handshake, and hello will make an impact on your guests. If your organization serves young people, have them be your greeters. Make sure they are dressed in similar attire (e.g., white or logo t-shirts, khaki pants). One group serving senior citizens has senior volunteers, each wearing a ribboned "Volunteer" badge, greeting people. Arts groups may have artists or patrons greeting people and thanking them for coming.

Another effective warm-up tool is music. There is nothing like music to put people in the mood before the event officially begins. A children's choir, a single vocalist, or a background tape can subtly set the tone. One rainforest preservation group set up their entire pre-event area as a rainforest, with sounds and smells and even some of the foliage of the rainforest. Their guests were thoroughly engaged and curious before the event even began.

Nametags

The first official stop before the guests arrive at their tables is the nametag table. Pre-printed nametags with each guest's table number are arranged alphabetically and set out at tables hosted by friendly volunteers. Guests pick up their own nametags and quickly move into the room, where they are shown right to their numbered table. The volunteers who work at the nametag table have been alerted to look for guests who are last-minute additions or substitutions and to send them to a designated table for such special exceptions.

At the end of the event, these volunteers collect the unclaimed nametags to be sure the event records reflect who did and did not attend. This helps you to be accurate in your follow-up.

Special Exceptions Table

The job of the quick-thinking volunteers at this table is to work as efficiently as possible to get each person into the room before the event begins. Unless you have several super-speedy computer stations set up to make nametags on the spot, hand-printed nametags will substitute just fine. Most tables for ten can accommodate twelve people. Have several (if not all) of your tables set for twelve so you can let the latecomers or surprise guests sit with their friends. This should not affect the number of meals you order; it just allows your guests a little more flexibility in seating.

The volunteers at this table should each be equipped with guest lists sorted both alphabetically and by table number, so they can quickly place people. Better yet, have one or two empty tables at the back of the room near the entry doors to encourage people to take a place there. Most latecomers or substitute guests won't mind being seated there, especially if you have a stand-in Table Captain from the organization who greets them.

These "back" tables are also ideal for your volunteers to sit at once their volunteer duties are done. That way they can enjoy the program they have worked so hard to produce and enjoy the meal as well. These tables also provide seating for representatives of the media who may choose to join you on late notice.

As detailed as it may seem, all of this advance planning will serve you well in all the excitement of the event day. Let's turn next to the people most essential to the success of your event—your Table Captains.

CHAPTER 10

TABLE CAPTAINS

Once you have made the commitment to put on the Free One-Hour Ask Event, scheduled the event, and booked your venue, your main focus will be on the recruitment and tending of your Table Captains.

From now until the event, your relationship with your Table Captains will follow our very structured Table Captain Timeline. This timeline should serve as a general overview of all of your main interactions with your Table Captains (see page 78).

CRITERIA FOR SELECTING YOUR TABLE CAPTAINS

The number one indicator of a great Table Captain is their passion for your organization. Number two is their ability to follow through with their invitations and actually fill their table with ten people on the day of the event. Number three is their ability to keep in touch with you. Will they respond to your e-mail messages and phone calls in a timely way? Will they keep in touch if they are falling behind on their invitations or if someone cancels at the last minute? These are the criteria you will wish you had paid better attention to as the event draws nearer.

TABLE CAPTAIN TIMELINE
FREE ONE-HOUR ASK EVENT

12 weeks out:
- All Table Captains confirmed

10 weeks out:
- Kick-off meeting/training—Distribute Table Captain packet, including:
  - Table Captain Welcome Letter
  - Sample script for inviting their guests
  - Table Captain Job Description
  - Guest List Form (with deadline)
  - Form to those unable to attend (to receive information or be invited to a Point of Entry)
  - 14 "Save the Date" postcards

  Optional:
  - FAQ's about the event
  - One-page overview of organization
  - Map/directions to the event site

6 – 8 weeks out:
- Table Captains invite their guests
- Mail "Save the Date" cards as guests confirm (or have Table Captains send them out weekly)

3 weeks out:
- Final Table Captain lists due

Ongoing:
- Send Table Captains updates about testimonials, video, attendance, etc. (via phone, fax, or e-mail)

2 – 3 days before:
- Table Captains contact their guests to confirm
- Mail out final Table Captain Bulletin

1 – 2 days before:
- Call Table Captains to confirm number of guests and give last minute event reminders (i.e. parking instructions, picking up packet on day of event, etc.)

Day of Event:
- Provide packet/envelope with pledge cards and return envelopes, welcome "how to do this" letter and pens

DETERMINING THE NUMBER OF TABLE CAPTAINS

Here is where you must be a realist. Use our tested formulas if you want to have every seat filled and avoid paying for extra meals. You must assume that at least 15% of your Table Captains will not come through at all. In other words, they will agree to be a Table Captain and yet, on the day of the event, they will not have any guests. In fact, they may not even attend the event themselves. They are not bad people; they meant well when they accepted the assignment, but, for whatever reason, they were unable to deliver. Plan for this 15% Table Captain attrition; do not be surprised by it on event day.

Then you need to figure that, for the Table Captains who do come through, at least 15% of their guests will not attend. Although they will have received two check-in calls from their Table Captain in the week before the event, on the day of the event, for one reason or another, people will be unable to attend. A sick child, a medical emergency, or the weather—factor this percentage into your numbers.

In other words, if you want your Ask Event to have 200 guests, you will need to start with twenty-seven Table Captains—which is quite a lot more than the twenty Table Captains you might have anticipated. By the time you allow for 15% of the Table Captains who will not fulfill their role, you are down to twenty-three Table Captains. Then when you allow for 15% of the remaining guests who will not show up, you will barely have your 200 people. Again, be a realist and don't be left paying for uneaten meals and losing pledges from the guests who could have taken those empty seats.

WHERE TO FIND YOUR TABLE CAPTAINS

Knowing how many Table Captains you will need to get to your goal, you should start with a list of twice as many potential Table Captains. Sticking with our 200-person event example, you would need twenty-seven times two, or fifty-four potential people you could ask to become Table Captains.

Where can you look to find those fifty-four people?

I recommend you turn to your Treasure Map, the diagram you have made to identify those groups like your board, staff, volunteers, vendors, neighbors, schools, faith organizations, doctors, etc., who would naturally want to know more about your organization. (See page 215 for instructions on creating a Treasure Map.)

Identify as many potential Table Captains as you can from each group on your Treasure Map. If, for example, you have a strong volunteer program with many roles for volunteers, you might want to have one Table Captain from each type of volunteer: for example, the volunteer drivers, the volunteers who serve lunches, and the hospital volunteers who deliver the flowers. These natural groups will make ideal Ask Event guests, and there is no doubt at least one leader within each group (sometimes more, if it is a large group) who would not want their group to miss out on the event. Be sure to let them know in the invitation process if you will be mentioning their program in any way.

For interfaith groups, each church or synagogue or mosque that sends a team of volunteers to help out each week at the shelter or meals program also becomes a natural group for one Table Captain to host.

In other words, as you select your Table Captains, be sure to look at the *groups*, and not just the individuals that your organization interacts with.

There will be certain board members who will naturally make great Table Captains, and others who should be invited to sit at the board/VIP table. Do not pressure your board members to become Table Captains—it won't work. Far better to let them come, if they choose, to see the event firsthand. Conversely, you also need to allow for the board members who will fill multiple tables. At the school where the model was developed, we had one board member at our first event fill six tables.

What about staff members as Table Captains? Here is another one of our formulas: no more than 5-10% of your Table Captains should be staff. Therefore, for a 200-person Ask Event, out of your starting twenty-seven Table Captains, no more than three should be staff.

The more diversity and breadth of your community represented at your Ask Event, the better. Choose Table Captains from each group on your Treasure Map. If your organization works with lawyers, doctors, teachers, and parents, you should have Table Captains from each of those groups.

Make sure that each Table Captain—even those insiders who already know your organization's work—has attended a Point of Entry Event before the Ask Event.

That leads us to a final source of Table Captains, one that often gets overlooked in the initial planning stages for the event: Point of Entry guests. Do not underestimate the power of your Point of Entry to convert a first-time attendee into a potential Table Captain.

INVITING PEOPLE TO BE TABLE CAPTAINS

Now that you've decided who you want to invite, how do you go about actually inviting them?

A suggested script for you to use as you invite people to become Table Captains is included on page 82.

THE TABLE CAPTAIN KICK-OFF MEETING

Following our Table Captain Timeline (page 78), you should have all your Table Captains recruited by twelve weeks prior to the event. Next on the Table Captain Timeline, now that you have recruited twenty-seven enthusiastic and willing Table Captains, is to educate them about their responsibilities. This is best done at a Table Captain kick-off meeting, held ten weeks prior to the Ask Event. The purpose of this one-hour meeting is to rally the troops and get everyone excited about the Ask Event.

A sample agenda for the kick-off event is included on page 83.

Kick-off Attendance

Here is another essential dose of reality and a major pitfall to be avoided: in spite of the time you put into planning the kick-off meeting, you should expect that only 50-60% of your Table Captains will attend. You will need to meet personally or by phone with each Table

SAMPLE TABLE CAPTAIN INVITATION SCRIPT

FREE ONE-HOUR ASK EVENT

You have been a good friend to our organization and a real supporter of our mission. You have invited many people to attend our one-hour getting-to-know-us tours. I'd like to invite you to consider participating in a new way with us—by being a Table Captain at our upcoming fundraising breakfast.

This event is different from other events we have done in the past.

- The goal of the event is to raise unrestricted funds for our programs and to spread our message in the community.
- It's totally free.
- It will only be an hour long.
- There will be no requirement that anyone give at the event.
- It will be our job to inspire people so that they will want to give.
- As much as anything, we want people to come and find out about the great work we do.
- It will make you proud to be involved with us.

Each Table Captain is asked to fill a table of ten people by inviting them personally. They can be friends, coworkers, family, neighbors, anybody you know. We ask that at least two of your guests be people who have already attended our _____ (*Point of Entry*) tours. The others may have heard about us before, or maybe this is their first introduction. Your job is to get them to attend. You do not have to ask anyone for money.

Here are the details (date and time) of the event.

Would you help us by being a Table Captain for our event?

If yes: Great! Thanks! We'll have a special meeting for Table Captains on _____ (*date*) to go over all the details. If you can't make it to the meeting, we'll give you a packet with all the information you need. We'll also have reminder cards for you to give to people you invite. If they'd like to find out more about us before the event, we have several _____ (*Point of Entry Events*) scheduled that they could attend.

Please make sure you invite and confirm enough people for the table to be filled. Expect two to four people to cancel, so we recommend confirming twelve to fourteen people, to make sure ten will be there. Thanks again! You will have a great time, and you'll be very proud of us!

If maybe or need to consider: When will you know? Is there any more information you need? Can I get back to you?

If no: Thanks for considering it. I'm sorry you won't be able to be a Table Captain. Of course, we'd love to have you come as a guest to the event, even if you're not a Table Captain, and bring anyone else you'd like. Is there anyone else who comes to mind who we should ask to be a Table Captain?

If they have a time conflict for the event: Would you like to help in the planning/preparation for the event? We'd love to have your input.

TABLE CAPTAIN KICK-OFF AGENDA

FREE ONE-HOUR ASK EVENT

Welcome *(Exec. Director)* 3 minutes	Thank people for attending and explain the importance of the Ask Event and their essential role in its success.
Introductions *(Exec. Director)* 10 minutes	Introduce your team and your Team Leader who will be coordinating the event. Introduce any board members in attendance. Then take time for each person to introduce themselves and state how they are connected to the organization, including why they care about the organization.
Overview of the Raising More Money Model *(Team Leader/ Devel. Director)* 5 minutes	Using handouts of the model or a flip chart, the Team Leader explains the four steps of the model and where the Ask Event fits into the larger process of cultivating lifelong relationships with mission-focused donors.
Ask Event Program Overview *(Team Leader/ Devel. Director)* 10 minutes	The person responsible for the event walks everyone through the program for the event, step by step. Take questions as you go through this.
Treasure Map for the Organization *(Team Leader/ Devel. Director)* 5 minutes	Draw out a quick Treasure Map on a flip chart or overhead projector, or show them the Treasure Map your team has already prepared. Highlight the many groups that already know about your work and might want to attend the event, including the group called "Point of Entry Guests," many of whom have now been cultivated and are ready to be asked to contribute financially.
Personal Treasure Map for Each Table Captain *(Team Leader/ Devel. Director)* 10 minutes	Have each Table Captain make a personal Treasure Map of the people they come into contact with on a regular basis, in their work or personal lives. Be sure to cover what resources these people have in abundance and what might be their self-interest in learning more about the organization. End by having each Table Captain make a list of at least 30 people from their personal Treasure Map they could invite to sit at their table at the Ask Event. People often become very excited at this point. They bring out their address books and personal planners. Be prepared for some people to tell you that they would like to host more than one table—this should be a natural outcome of this part of the kick-off agenda.
Table Captain Packet Review *(Team Leader/ Devel. Director)* 5 minutes	Hand out the Table Captain packets and walk people through the contents. Be sure to include how you will stay in contact with the Table Captains from now until the day of the event, either by phone, fax, or e-mail. Let them know you will be contacting them often.
Questions *(Team Leader/ Exec. Director)* 10 minutes	Give people plenty of time to ask questions. You want them to leave the kick-off reconnected to their passion for the organization and excited and confident about the Ask Event and their role in it.
Thank You and Close *(Exec. Director)* 1 minute	Be sure to take the time to tell your Table Captains how much you appreciate them. Tell them how you will be in touch with them from now until the day of the event.

Total time: 56 minutes

Captain who is unable to attend the kick-off, and walk them through the Table Captain Packet, page by page, in order to make sure they understand how the event works and what is expected of them.

For those Table Captains who do not attend the kick-off, merely sending them the packet of materials they missed at the meeting will not suffice. We hear far too many upsetting stories of the problems caused by Table Captains who said yes to being a Table Captain, not understanding the unique nature of this event, thinking it was like other fundraising events they had "filled tables" for in the past. They did not invite their guests properly by using the specific wording to inform guests in advance that they would be asked to give money at the end of the event, etc.

Without a special meeting to go over the packet, your busy Table Captains may not open it until it is too late, leaving you with angry guests who have not been told in advance how the event works and—perhaps worse—embarrassed Table Captains.

While this may seem obvious, it is so often missed that it bears repeating: Any Table Captain who is unable to attend the Table Captain kick-off must receive a full (thirty-minute) briefing in-person —not with a secretary—or over the phone to cover every item in the Table Captain Packet that has been sent to them.

SCRIPT FOR TABLE CAPTAINS TO USE WHEN INVITING GUESTS

Because you will be relying so heavily on your Table Captains to invite each guest and to convey the mission-centered, no-pressure atmosphere of the Ask Event, it is essential that each Table Captain follow the same script as they invite people.

Be sure to stress to your Table Captains the importance of telling people in advance that they will be asked for money at the event, but that there is no obligation to give. (Recall that only 40-50% of the guests will give at the Ask Event; these numbers demonstrate that there will be no sense of pressure to give. Over 50% of the guests give no money at all on the day of the event.)

"Hello, _____, I'd like to invite you to join me at my table at the _____ event. This is a free breakfast for people to come and learn more about our organization. Yes, it is a fundraiser, too. You will be asked to consider making a contribution. There is no minimum and no maximum gift requested. It will be the job of the organization to inspire people to want to give. As much as anything, we want people to come and find out about the great programs offered. I would be delighted if you could join me."

FILLING TABLES

The Table Captains' focus during the ten weeks between the kick-off meeting and the Ask Event should be on filling their tables and inviting potential guests to Point of Entry Events. Some Table Captains will get right to work after the kick-off and have their tables filled two months before the event. They may even jump in and offer to host a Point of Entry Event for their friends. Others will take their time. And at least 15% will not do anything at all.

This process can be frustrating for seasoned event planners accustomed to controlling every aspect of an event, because so much is riding on its success. Unlike traditional fundraising events where guests are invited via formal invitations with a centralized RSVP process, the success of the Free One-Hour Ask Event is due primarily to the power of the personal invitation, delivered word-of-mouth, in-person, by telephone, or in a personal e-mail from a trusted friend.

Once you realize the extent to which you will be relying on your Table Captains, you will see why it is worth taking great care to select the very best people to fulfill this role.

Having said that, this does not mean that the event coordinator and others planning the event should back away from the invitation process; in fact, quite the opposite. Your job is to manage the invitation and table-filling process, albeit somewhat indirectly.

WEEKLY COMMUNICATION WITH TABLE CAPTAINS

We recommend you have one person accountable for communicating with your Table Captains weekly. Most groups do this by e-mail. They put out some type of informal weekly newsletter-style "event countdown" update, or just send a personal e-mail from the event coordinator, copying all the Table Captains. This includes news about the program, the venue, your new video, the people who have agreed to be Testimonial Speakers at the event, and the like. Each update should start off with the number of weeks left until the event and the number of weeks until their guest lists are due. Keep stressing this guest list deadline in all of your materials.

SAVE-THE-DATE CARDS

During this time, Table Captains should be sending out the Save-the-Date cards provided in their Table Captain Packets. Some organizations prefer to manage the Save-the-Date card process centrally as a way to have a clearer sense of the total number of guests invited to date. Doing this also gives the event coordinator a reason to call the Table Captains periodically to ask if there is anyone a Save-the-Date card should be mailed to.

If you have taken the 15% Table Captain attrition and 15% guest attrition rates into consideration in your planning, and you have recruited passionate Table Captains (with a maximum of 10% staff members as Table Captains), the process should work according to the recipe. You should be able to trust your Table Captains to manage sending out the Save-the-Date cards you have provided them—with personal notes to each guest—and to submit their guest lists to you according to our timeline, three weeks before the event.

THREE WEEKS OUT: FINAL TABLE CAPTAIN LISTS DUE

Hold firm to this deadline. Require your Table Captains to submit whatever list they have twenty-one days before the event, even if their table is only partially full. This will allow you to take stock of how much work is yet to be done with "slower" Table Captains and to get that work done.

On the twentieth day before your event, call every single Table Captain who submitted a partial list or no list at all. Ask the hard questions to determine how many guests they will actually have before the event. Factor a 15-20% attrition rate into the numbers they tell you. Begin looking at how you can consolidate tables. Rather than have struggling Table Captains back away from the job altogether, ask if they can fill half a table. Offer to pair them with another Table Captain they may know.

If they say they do not want to be a Table Captain at all, "bless and release" them graciously, invite them to attend the event anyway, and offer to seat them with someone else they know or at one of the VIP tables that your organization will be putting together. After all, if they care enough to have agreed to be a Table Captain originally, they wouldn't want to miss the event themselves!

As the lists arrive, begin entering the guest names and contact information into your database tracking system. This will save work after the event.

MAKING SURE EVERYONE GETS INVITED

By now, some of you may be wondering: What about all the people who might not be invited by a Table Captain? This is an important question.

To be sure that no one who would like to attend the event is inadvertently excluded, make a list of these key people, including all prior Point of Entry guests, prior donors, former board members, volunteers, corporate sponsors, and anyone else in the community who has asked to learn more.

Next, have your board and staff members review this list to determine the best person to call each of these guests. The inviter should be someone with whom the guest has a personal relationship. Then have the identified inviters invite the guests on their lists, following the same process as the Table Captain process: telephone or in-person invitation, "Save-the-Date" card mailed, and reminder call made two to three days before the event.

At the event, these special people can be seated in various places:

- At staff or board tables (it is fine for them to fill more than one table).
- At a special VIP table.
- Matched up with someone they know.
- At tables where a Table Captain is having difficulty filling his/her table (be sure to tell the appropriate Table Captain that this guest will be joining them).

TWO WEEKS OUT:
FINAL TABLE CAPTAIN BULLETIN

FINAL TABLE CAPTAIN BULLETIN
FREE ONE-HOUR ASK EVENT

(To be mailed out two weeks before Ask Event day)

DREAM BUILDER EVENT - FINAL DETAILS

The week before the event:

Please call each of your guests to reconfirm their attendance. Go over the details: date, time, and location. Since the event will be brief, please emphasize that we will start and end on time. Be sure they allow enough time to park and get to the room.

The morning of the event:

1. Please plan to arrive no later than _____ (30 minutes before the official start time).

2. Come to the special table marked "Table Captain Sign-In" to pick up your packet.

3. Go into the ballroom (early) to locate your table. Your table number will be on your nametag and on your packet envelope.

4. Greet your guests as they arrive.

5. Enjoy the program!

6. Near the end of the program, _____ will let you know when to pass out the pledge cards, envelopes, and pens. Please wait for those instructions. Please set an example for your guests by filling out your own pledge card at that time.

7. At the end of the event, be sure to collect the completed pledge cards and envelopes and replace them in the packet envelope.

8. Return your packet to the volunteers standing at the door as you leave the ballroom. We will be counting up the contributions immediately following the event and want to be sure to include all the tables.

ENJOY THE EVENT, AND THANK YOU AGAIN FOR MAKING IT POSSIBLE FOR _____ TO EXPAND OUR WORK IN THE COMMUNTY.

THE FINAL COUNTDOWN

2-3 days out: Table Captains reconfirm their guests individually by telephone or e-mail, telling them how much they are looking forward to seeing the guest at the event. They should not leave a message; they need to personally connect with each guest to hear that they will be attending.

1-2 days out: Call every Table Captain to reconfirm their final number of guests and review last-minute details, including what time to arrive, where to park, and a reminder to pick up their Table Captain envelope when they arrive at the event.

Day of Event: Have a separate sign-in table for Table Captains, hosted by someone who has been working with the Table Captains and/or is familiar with their names and lists. Greet them warmly and give them their large, brightly colored envelopes which contain a list of their duties for the day, ten pledge cards, ten small envelopes (one for each pledge card), and ten pens. Tell them how and where the larger envelope (filled with pledge cards) will be collected at the end of the event.

Now we are ready to turn to the program.

CHAPTER 11

PROGRAM OVERVIEW

If you have followed the recipe up until this point, you are ready to plan your one-hour program. In this chapter, we will walk through each program element, for an overview of the flow. The next few chapters will examine each of the main program components in more depth. As with everything else in the recipe, do not be tempted to deviate from these specifications.

As we have said, this event is choreographed like a theatrical production and every single one of your sixty minutes counts.

We have already covered the pre-event warm up—the greeters and music, the nametag table, and escorting people to their tables. There, guests are greeted by their friend the Table Captain and take their seats. There is an air of excitement.

PROGRAM ELEMENTS
Welcome and Thank You—3 minutes

The event begins at exactly the designated start time with a welcome and thank you from the board chair or emcee, someone who has a direct connection to the organization. Even if you are fortunate enough to have a professional media person agree to emcee your event, make sure that they have a personal reason for caring about the work of your organization.

Do not expect everyone to be in their seats waiting for the event

PROGRAM

FREE ONE-HOUR ASK EVENT

(Background music as guests arrive)

WELCOME & THANK YOU

3 minutes; board chair or emcee thanks board members, Table Captains, visiting dignitaries

OPENING EMOTIONAL HOOK

3 minutes; invocation, short video or audio PSA, song

EAT AND SOCIALIZE

10 minutes; emcee calls attention to centerpieces or vignettes/fact sheets in programs and to the souvenirs being passed around

VISIONARY LEADER

5 minutes; past, present, and future—facts and emotion; what's unique about the organization and why it needs support; creates the gap

VIDEO

7 minutes; emotion!

TESTIMONIALS

1 or 2 different perspectives; 3 minutes each; facts and inspiration, credibility; may use interview format

PITCH

7 minutes; no long speeches; someone credible walks the audience through the pledge card (includes time for guests to fill out the card and pass in to the Table Captain); no background music

WRAP UP

1 minute; emcee thanks them again for their support

(Background music plays as soon as event officially ends)

to begin. There will still be many empty seats. Tempted as you may be to delay due to low attendance at the start time, do not start late. It will throw off the timing of the entire event. The script for the welcome includes thanking the board members, Table Captains, and any special guests. This takes about three minutes, during which time many more guests will arrive.

Opening Emotional Hook—3 minutes

While the term "Emotional Hook" may sound crass, this element is essential to the program. It is designed to connect people emotionally to your mission within the first five minutes of the event. You want your guests to know right away that you have something meaningful and important to tell them about; you did not just invite them to have breakfast. This opening Emotional Hook could be a child reading a poem, a candle-lighting ceremony, someone singing a song related to the mission, or an inspiring invocation. One domestic violence group played a recording of a 911 emergency call, and another group showed the video of their new thirty-second public service announcement. The opening Emotional Hook sets the tone for the entire event; it wakes people up to your mission and piques their interest for more.

Eat and Socialize—10 minutes

This is the only "down time" in the one-hour program. People need a few minutes to socialize and connect with a few of the people at their table. The emcee has told them the program will start back up in ten minutes and encouraged them to look at their table tents (folded-over pieces of paper) in front of each person's place, displaying something that personalizes the work of the organization and educates people about the mission. For example, one American Lung Association event had photos of kids at asthma camp with stories by each child of why they look forward all year long to going to asthma camp. Other groups have cards with statistics about diseases of the eye, or percentages of various toxic chemicals contained in certain foods.

People are encouraged to pass these cards around so others can learn from them as well.

This social time is also the part of the program where the guests receive their gifts, delivered personally to their tables by a volunteer, program participant, or family member. Again, the purpose is not to give people a valuable object, but rather to connect them to the work of the organization even during this ten minutes of down time. Think about what you could give people that would tie into your program and your mission and how it could be delivered or presented to them as they sit at their tables.

For example, the same event that had the stories about asthma camp had camp-aged kids passing around plastic straws in beautiful little cellophane bags with bows. Later in the program, the guests were asked to squeeze the straws until they were partially closed and then inhale through them, to experience what it feels like to have an asthma attack.

One group serving homebound rural elderly individuals passed out holiday greeting cards and pens and asked the event guests to write a card to one of the people they serve. Other gifts may be less experiential, like apples, pens, bookmarks, pins, and buttons.

Visionary Leader Talk—5 minutes

Now it is time for the leader of the organization to share the vision for the future. The Visionary Leader Talk is the anchor element of your Ask Event. It is worth taking the time to craft it carefully and to rehearse it several times, coaching your Visionary Leader to deliver the talk powerfully, following the script.

Every organization has a Visionary Leader. This is usually the executive director or founder, if the founder is still active in the day-to-day operations of the organization. If the organization does not have paid staff, the board chair generally serves as the Visionary Leader. While you may think your Visionary Leader does not always sound visionary or, conversely, may sound *too* visionary for most people, there is a way to craft a Visionary Leader Talk for every organization.

The Visionary Leader Talk at the Ask Event lasts five minutes. It tells people about the past, present, and future of the organization, and it clearly conveys "the gap" between where your organization is now and where you need to go in order to fulfill the next phase of your mission. This talk is delivered with emotion.

Chapter 12 goes into more detail about the content and delivery of the Visionary Leader Talk.

Video—7 minutes

A video is essential at your Ask Event. We refer to this as a seven-minute, "three-cry" video. This is because the main job of the video is to inspire people about the human impact of your work and move them to tears. It brings to light, in an emotional way, the deeper work of the organization. People should be noticeably moved, not necessarily because they feel sad or upset, but because they have been touched. Perhaps the video made them laugh, or reminded them of all they have to be thankful for. First and foremost, then, the video must move people.

Most groups err on the side of too little emotion, feeling it is unprofessional or in some way insulting to the people they serve or the work they do. However, emotion is so key to fundraising that most people are not even conscious of the degree to which their emotions drive their charitable giving. If you don't capture people's hearts as well as their minds, you will never have lifelong donors.

While there will be several other emotional aspects of the Ask Event program, including the Visionary Leader Talk and the testimonials, your program must also include a powerful, succinct, emotionally riveting video shown on a large screen in a big room with the lights turned down. People will feel the impact right in their chairs.

Chapter 13 addresses how to produce the seven-minute video, what to include, and some thoughts for funding production costs.

Testimonials—6 minutes

There is no substitute for a live testimonial. A firsthand account of how your organization changed a life is the most powerful statement of the impact of your work. It must leave people so deeply moved and reminded of what is truly important in life that they feel compelled to take action.

We allow a maximum of six minutes for the testimonial(s) at the Ask Event. There are several options for how to use this time. Most groups have one or—at the most—two Testimonial Speakers. Other groups prefer to use this time to interview three or four people with specific prepared interview questions.

The ideal Testimonial Speaker is someone who has had a first-hand experience of your organization's work—a client or family member, a long time arts lover, or one or two alumni of your school or program.

The testimonial talk follows a prescribed outline with three main parts: what life was like before this person became involved with the organization; what services or intervention the organization offered that changed things for the person; and what life is like now, including how this person is able to give back to others.

You will need to script and rehearse your Testimonial Speakers to be sure they speak passionately and stay within their allocated time.

Chapter 14 covers many issues related to Testimonial Speakers, including how to choose your Testimonial Speaker(s), rehearsing and caring for your speakers, and other contingency issues.

Pitch—7 minutes

The Ask Event culminates in the Pitch. It is now fifty minutes into the sixty-minute program. People have been warned this is coming. They know they are going to be asked for money. At this point, 40-50% of the people are ready to give. They want to know how to go about making a financial contribution right now. The remaining 50-60% of the people are not ready to give at the event. They may end up giving the next day, the next week, or the next year. They may want to go home and talk it over with others, come to a Point of Entry themselves or with others, transfer money or property, or meet with the board or committee. Or they may decide not to get involved with your organization at all. They may have other issues they are more involved with at this time.

The job of the Pitch Person at the Ask Event is to focus on the people who are ready to give and to tell them how to go about that.

The Pitch Person should not be trying to convince the majority who have already decided not to give today. We refer to the Pitch Person as a "credible, school teacher-like" person: "credible" because they are truly tied to the organization's mission, and "school teacher-like" because they will follow a script. They understand that their job is to walk people through the pledge card and help them to give. They understand that they have a very specific and critical job to do.

The Pitch Person tells the Table Captains when to pass out the pledge cards, envelopes, and pens to each guest. After walking the audience through each line on the pledge sheet, instructing them how to fill out the form, and giving them time to do that, the Pitch Person directs the guests to pass their envelopes back to the Table Captain.

The Table Captains have another essential role during the Pitch. They must set the example for their guests by filling out their pledge cards at this time. Even if the Table Captains have already made a financial contribution to the organization, they need to be writing *something* on their pledge cards during the pitch. The guests will glance at the Table Captains and follow their lead.

Chapter 15 covers the pitch script, sample pledge card, and how to choose the ideal Pitch Person.

Wrap up—1 minute

The emcee or board chair thanks everyone for coming and for their support for the organization. People are invited to linger and chat if they like. The background music comes on and the event ends, right on time, in sixty minutes.

REHEARSING

To improve the likelihood that your program will flow smoothly and that each element will be strong and effective unto itself, it is essential to have a full rehearsal of the event program one to three days prior to the event, in the actual location where the event will take place.

Let's look next in more detail at the Visionary Leader Talk.

CHAPTER 12

THE VISIONARY LEADER TALK

The Visionary Leader Talk is the anchor element of your Ask Event program. It needs to be carefully scripted and delivered powerfully, from the heart. It lets people know that the Visionary Leader is serious about fulfilling on the mission of the organization.

WHO DELIVERS THE VISIONARY LEADER TALK

People need to hear the vision directly from the passionate leader of the organization. At the Ask Event, your Visionary Leader will be your executive director. If you do not have an executive director, the most senior staff member delivers this talk. If there are no staff at all, the talk is delivered by the board chair or top-ranking volunteer leader. Do not deviate and choose another "more-visionary-sounding" person who is involved with your organization or a well-recognized speaker from the larger community. This needs to be someone in an official position of leadership.

While your Visionary Leader certainly must be credible and able to speak intelligently on the critical issues facing your organization, the main job of this talk is to inspire people about the urgent nature of the mission. After all, this person is the one in charge—the person at the helm to steer the ship to the next destination. Who else would we look to for vision and inspiration? The Visionary Leader's true passion and emotion about the organization's work must come through. If the Visionary Leader can't get passionate about it, why should we?

THIS TALK IS DIFFERENT

Most Visionary Leaders are very passionate people, yet when asked to speak about their organizations, they often default to the type of speech they would give to civic or community groups—namely, an impressive, twenty-minute, stand-alone speech about the programs and services of the organization and some of the challenges it is currently facing.

Unlike talks given to civic groups, the Visionary Leader Talk at the Ask Event is highly crafted and spoken from the heart. It does not need to stand alone; it is delivered in the midst of a one-hour program that is solely about your organization. This is *your* show, and people are expecting to be inspired by the Visionary Leader. There are many other elements of the program to complement this talk.

The Visionary Leader Talk at the Ask Event lasts just five minutes, and it follows the same basic outline as the Visionary Leader Talk given at your Point of Entry Events (see page 102), about the history and the dreams of the organization.

The best way to begin this talk is to trace the organization's history in a sentence or two. What year did you get started? What underlying values were your founders committed to? What were the most challenging issues and concerns facing the organization? Cite some myth-buster facts about how much the problem and the issues may have changed over the years. Yet what organization is better prepared than yours to address today's issues?

The Visionary Leader Talk should also include a personal story. People naturally want to know how the leader got involved with this organization and to hear the one story that always reconnects this person to the organization's work.

Be sure that this talk identifies "the gap" between where the organization is now and where it needs to go to fulfill the next phase of its mission. "One of the hardest jobs for our staff is turning away the people we can't serve. There were over 200 of them last month alone." Cite examples of the additional programs that could be offered, additional people that could be served, more children edu-cated, or more lives saved.

"Looking out to the future, we see many more challenges, as well as many great opportunities that could come our way. Here's how we are planning to deal with those. Here are the great unknowns. While the task may seem daunting to some, we have a vision for how to meet the needs and challenges and how to take advantage of the opportu-nities. After all, this is our mission; it's what we're here for."

CONCERNS ABOUT YOUR VISIONARY LEADER

Many groups have concerns about asking their Visionary Leader to deliver this talk. They feel the executive director is not a strong speaker or, perhaps, not even very visionary these days.

However, you must give this person a speaking role at the Ask Event, even if it is a brief one. Without that, people will wonder: Who is the leader of this great organization and why didn't we hear from that person? One option is to divide the Visionary Leader Talk into two talks. Have the executive director speak for a minute or two, perhaps sharing a story. You can then have the board chair speak about the past, present, and future of the organization, conveying a clear sense of "the gap," as well as the plan, even loosely defined for filling that gap. Then have them share the dreams for the future of the organization.

Know, too, that the experience of delivering this talk to a large audience of people who have come to hear about your organization is a very emotional moment for any Visionary Leader. In our rehearsal coaching calls, we tell the Visionary Leader to expect to be moved when they come up to the podium and look out into the audience.

PASSION IS THE KEY

As with every speaker at your Ask Event, the single most impor-tant element of the Visionary Leader Talk is that a genuine passion for the work of the organization must come through. People need to see that this person is dedicated to the fulfillment of the organization's mission. People are coming to your Ask Event to be inspired and connected to your work. They want to know that, should they choose

VISIONARY LEADER TALK OUTLINE

I. BRIEF HISTORY OF THE ORGANIZATION
- When was it founded?
- By whom?
- How has it evolved and grown since then?

II. MISSION AND UNDERLYING PHILOSOPHY
- Why does the organization really exist?
- What values does it teach, encourage, or represent?

III. TOP THREE PROGRAMS AND SERVICES OFFERED
- What is the simplest way to categorize/cluster your programs so a new person can understand what you do? (Do not try to include all programs in the list.)
- What programs might people be least aware of or surprised by?

IV. "MYTH-BUSTER" STATISTICS
- How does the population you serve differ from what people would expect?
- How does the problem differ from people's perceptions?
- What is the extent of the need in the community?

V. THE GAP
- What will it take for you to fulfill your mission?
- How many people are unserved or underserved now?
- What is the impact to society of the absence of those needed programs and services?

VI. A STORY
- What keeps you working there?
- What one story always reconnects you to the importance of your work?

VII. VISION FOR THE FUTURE
- Where do you want to be five to ten years from now?
- How much closer to fulfilling that mission will you be?
- How many more people will benefit?
- What is the simple overview of your plan for getting there?

to make a financial contribution, they will be investing in an organization with strong visionary leadership.

For examples of Visionary Leader Talks from groups that were trained and coached by Raising More Money, see the Samples, page 171.

CHAPTER 13

THE SEVEN-MINUTE VIDEO

The seven-minute video is a required element of the Ask Event program. As we have said, its main purpose is to evoke emotion—it literally has got to move people to tears three times.

While you certainly want the video to educate people about your work, it is far more important that it inspire and move them. Remember that this video is only one element of your Ask Event program. There are many other places in the program to educate your audience.

This is not meant to be a generic, stand-alone video that tells everyone everything about your organization. In fact, it may not cover the details of your work at all.

The challenge in producing a great seven-minute video is synthesizing your work down to its essence. That usually means boiling it down to your organization's impact on the lives of real people. After all, real people will be watching your video. Real people will be giving money to your organization. Remember: As individuals, we are emotional donors looking for rational reasons to justify our emotional decision to give. If the guests at your event are not moved and inspired about your work, they will not be likely to give.

There are many other media that can be used effectively to educate and inspire people—PowerPoint presentations, slides, overhead transparencies, even audiotape. But when it comes to evoking emotion, nothing quite compares to a professionally made video. An example of this is television news. In the space of one to two minutes, a great news story gives you facts you can remember, the emotion of real human beings, action film footage, and sound. Imagine, then, what you will be able to accomplish in seven minutes!

PRODUCING YOUR VIDEO

There are only two requirements of your video in the Raising More Money Model: it should be no longer than seven minutes and it must move people to tears three times.

Let's look at some ways you could accomplish that.

Probably the easiest and least expensive method is to edit video footage that has already been made about your organization. If you are fortunate enough to have had a television story done on your organization, it is likely that at least part of it captured the essence of your work. Perhaps they interviewed one of your staff members, volunteers, or a consumer of your services. In this case, they will probably have focused on some aspect of your programming that represents one of the core aspects of your mission. You could, for example, use only the testimonial or interview footage and splice it together with your own video material that speaks to your larger mission. Or you could add in two other testimonials or stories about other programs you offer, or other aspects of your work.

Perhaps your organization is part of a larger national organization or network of organizations that address a particular issue. Rather than going to the expense of making your own video, use all or part of what already exists. Often, the national office will have produced an excellent video, using generic examples, which is suitable for customizing to your region. In that case, decide which elements you want to showcase locally, and have your video producer edit the national footage right into your locally produced video.

In our workshops, we often recommend that the headquarters of national organizations catalog all their video footage so that local chapters can select the types of testimonials that best meet their needs, topically and demographically. This way, local chapters can pick and choose just what they need, saving costly duplication across chapters.

In the case of a national health organization, for example, they could catalog and index video footage of testimonials from patients, doctors, and family members of varying ages and ethnic backgrounds.

Whether you will be using existing footage or starting from scratch, producing a video will force you to figure out how to tell your complicated story in a succinct, emotional fashion. This can be a significant challenge.

I strongly recommend that you engage a professional video producer, someone who has a track record of making this type of video. Take the time to find the right person. Most nonprofit organizations have someone associated with them who can help get a video made. Perhaps it is a person in the training department of a local corporation, a friend in the TV newsroom, or a student at a local college. Finding a person to donate their services to produce a video may not be that difficult. The challenge is to find someone who can make this particular type of video.

PRODUCTION COSTS

Think twice before you accept a generous offer for donated video production; these offers usually come with strings attached. Once you have accepted such an offer, it becomes difficult to critique the work or request the number of edits that may be necessary to get what you want. All too often, we find groups who end up with a video that is only 75% of what they wanted, because it was too difficult to deal in a straightforward manner with the pro-bono video producer.

The best and simplest way to get the video you want is to pay an expert to produce it for you. Current costs, depending on where you are located, range from $1,000 to $1,500 per finished minute. That means you should expect to pay as much as $10,000 for the final product.

Before you discard the notion of paying a professional to do the job, consider the many sources of funding available to you. First and most likely, you could apply for a grant from a local foundation or corporation—ideally one that already knows and appreciates your work. Make your case for the long-term value of having a top-quality video. In your proposal, explain why it is difficult to showcase your work firsthand (if it is) or why you feel the video is needed at your Ask Event.

Next, consider asking one donor to fund the cost of producing your video. One organization that participated in our workshop went to a grateful parent of a child whose life had been turned around by their fine work. The donor was delighted to fund the video, saying that they would do whatever they could to help spread the word so that other parents would not have to suffer. The organization gave credit to the donor at the end of the video—and it just happened to work out so that the donor's child's testimonial worked perfectly into the script!

Finally, do not overlook the possibility of paying for the video out of your budget. When you think of the hundreds of times it will be used, your investment will be well worth it. Many groups pay for the production costs from their own budgets and then have copies of their video donated by a corporation or individual donor. These copies are given to everyone who attends their Ask Event, or people who become founding members of their Multiple-Year Giving Society, or even to people who were unable to attend the event. For the nominal duplication cost, your message can be widely disseminated and yield great results. While they may not read a book or even a brochure, most people will watch a video if it is given to them.

WHAT TO INCLUDE

Given the complex array of programs and services your organization offers, do not surrender the strategic decisions about video content to the producer. While their outsider perspective will be invaluable in making sense of your work to "real" people, it is your responsibility to make sure that they see and understand enough of what you do so that they have the full picture before they decide what to include and how to spin it.

Think of your standard litany of programs—the one you can recite in your sleep, the list you tell people whenever they ask what your organization does. Odds are, that list is overkill for most people when recited verbally. Not only is it full of insider shorthand and jargon, but it would take too long to cover each of those programs even if everyone understood your language. Your job is to find the one umbrella theme or topic that includes all of your programs. This will probably be—of all things—your mission. After all, you wouldn't be offering this diverse range of programs and services if they didn't somehow fit naturally under that umbrella called your mission.

I recommend that the heart and soul of your video be your mission. Have someone—ideally the Visionary Leader or one of the beneficiaries of your service—say that mission out loud in the video. Then relate each program to it.

Choose no more than three programs to showcase in your video. Find a way to link them to your mission and to each other. For each program, tell a few facts and have a Testimonial Speaker share how their life has changed, thanks to that program. Thread them together with a narrator or main voice (often one of your own staff or board). Another way to accomplish this is by having the narrator ask the same questions of each Testimonial Speaker. Questions like: "What was your life like before you learned about this organization?" "How did you hear about it?" "What is your life like now?" "What would you like others to know about this organization?"

Consider the elements of your Emotional Hook as you prepare the video. For example, if nostalgia is part of what moves people about your organization, you might interview your Testimonial Speakers about their favorite memories of camp, a former counselor, or teacher. Think of what hooks you! It may not be as complicated as you would expect.

Beyond the images and the voices, the music you choose can make all the difference. Recently I previewed a video for a group in one of our workshops. The footage was spectacular. There were excellent close-up action shots of program participants deeply engaged in their work and stellar testimonials, but the music was choppy and annoying. By simply substituting warmer, richer music, the same footage evoked far more emotion—which ultimately led to larger gifts. This is another reason to work with a professional. They know the range of musical backgrounds available, and they should be able to offer you several selections to choose from.

TEST IT OUT

Finally, once you have refined the video to the point that you are satisfied with it, show it to several people who will tell you the truth. There is a good chance that it will need to be more emotional. Or perhaps people will tell you that it needs more factual content. While it may have moved them to tears, they still may not understand what your organization does or how some of the programs you offer fit together.

Two of my favorite videos were made very simply and on relatively low budgets. The first, put together by an organ donor organization, was a series of simple ten-second testimonials from organ donor recipients: "My life began again on May 10, 1993," spoken by a woman holding her baby, or the man on the golf course saying: "I got my new life on July 7, 1996." There were about twelve of these people who each quickly gave the date they got their new lease on life, thanks to a donated organ. The video also included a couple of people who were obviously quite debilitated, saying that every day they pray their phone will ring with the news that someone has donated the vital organ they need.

All the while, in the background of this video was simple, moving music. The video was about five minutes long, interspersed with still shots of facts: "X number of people received organ transplants last year. X number died because there was no organ available. You could make the difference. Sign up to be an organ donor today."

The last testimonial was a man holding his baby and saying, "Every day of my life since March 22, 1997, has been a gift. I thank the Organ Donor Program for the gift of my life every single morning."

Another outstanding video was produced by a school for children with learning disabilities. It started with shots in the classroom of teachers and students deeply engaged in learning, then shifted to short clips of parents and children, one at a time, looking straight into the camera, saying thank you to a particular teacher who had changed their life or the life of their child. Great music, clean footage, no huge budget, less than seven minutes. A great investment.

Consider this example as another effective use of video: One family service organization sent copies of their video with a bag of microwave popcorn and a letter to everyone who was unable to attend their Ask Event. The letter invited them to sit down with their family —popcorn included—and watch the video together. It included two or three questions they might want to ask after viewing it. The letter ended by saying the person writing the letter would like to give them a call in the next couple of weeks to get their feedback. With relatively little subsequent cultivation, many of these families became Multiple-Year Donors.

Remember, though, that these videos were only sent to people who had expressed a sincere interest in wanting to attend the Ask Event and were unable to make it at the last minute. The downside of this approach is that the seven-minute video, which was used as one element of the event program in between other live presenters, must now stand alone in the potential donor's home VCR. That is why the one-on-one follow-up is so important.

PRODUCTION TIME

Many groups use the lengthy lead-time needed to produce a video as an excuse for never making one. While more advance time for planning is best, most of the final shooting and editing can be done over a period of just a few days. We have worked with some groups that produce their entire video, start to finish, in less than two weeks' time, and others that take up to six months to plan and produce their video.

Take the time to think through the video strategy that fits for your organization. It will be part of the lasting legacy you will be leaving.

CHAPTER 14

THE TESTIMONIAL SPEAKER

The Testimonial Speaker is strategically placed in the program, sandwiched between the video and the final element in the Ask Event program, the Pitch. The testimonial underscores, in a subliminal way, all that has already been said in the program. This person attests to the fact that your work makes a huge difference in the lives of real people every day. These remarks are delivered in a straightforward and succinct manner and should touch people deeply.

CHOOSING YOUR TESTIMONIAL SPEAKERS

The ideal Testimonial Speaker is a grateful recipient of your programs or services who is comfortable speaking publicly and will follow a well-rehearsed script. Their story needs to represent a typical story of someone you serve, rather than the occasional exception.

The rainforest preservation group mentioned in an earlier chapter actually had one of the indigenous tribesmen flown in to speak personally on the impact of the organization's work on his tribe. While you may not want to go to that extreme, do consider the very best person to tell the story. The successful alumni of the inner-city after school program, the inspired opera patron, or even a staff member reading a letter from a former client can be extremely powerful. Even groups concerned about confidentiality will be surprised by the number of former clients who are ready and willing to tell their stories.

HOW THE TESTIMONIALS WORK

The total time allotted for testimonial talks is six minutes, but you do not have to use the entire allotted time. No individual talk should last longer than three minutes.

Each Testimonial Speaker's remarks should follow the same outline as the Essential Story that is told at your Point of Entry. This story has three stages or components:

Stage One is "Before." What was life like before I got involved with this organization? Paint the picture. Tell us the bad news.

Stage Two is the "Intervention." What brought me to the organization? What specific services and support were provided to me or my family? What did it feel like having people care about me?

Stage Three is "After." What are the results of the intervention? How has my life changed for the better? What is possible for me now? How am I now able to give back to the organization or to others?

For sample testimonials, see page 187.

HAVING MORE THAN ONE TESTIMONIAL SPEAKER

You only need one Testimonial Speaker at your Ask Event. More than one speaker can become repetitive and lose audience attention. Most groups have only one Testimonial Speaker.

Having said that, some groups insist on having more than one Testimonial Speaker. Sometimes this is because they want representatives of more than one of their programs. A large family service agency might have a testimonial from a young mother who came through their family shelter, as well as a man who was once a child in their residential treatment program. While it is true that each testimonial tends to showcase a different aspect of your work, that is not the purpose of these talks. Your video will have included three stories from people who have gone through your programs, each highlighting a different aspect, so the testimonials do not need to do that job.

Two Testimonial Speakers can create a "safety net" in case one speaker is weak. But two speakers can also throw off your sixty-minute timeline if one runs too long.

A "group testimonial" can be very effective if you can keep it within the six minutes allotted for testimonials. For example, a group serving adults with disabilities had several of their participants on the stage, in their wheelchairs, being interviewed round-robin style. Group Testimonial Speakers should know in advance and be well-prepared for the two or three questions they will be asked. In this case, they talked about how the organization had trained or retrained them in specific job skills and then helped them to find competitive employment. They talked about how good it felt to be living happy, "normal" lives on their own.

Seeing a group of your constituents gathered on the stage can make a big impact. Though the audience does not get to hear the full story of any one person, the composite effect is powerful.

HAVING CHILDREN AS TESTIMONIAL SPEAKERS

We do not recommend having children as your Testimonial Speakers, unless they are being interviewed with succinct questions from an adult they are comfortable with. Having a ten-year-old talk about how much he looked forward to asthma camp every year would never have flowed so smoothly if he had not been prompted along by these questions from his mom:

"What's your favorite thing about asthma camp?"

"What did you learn at asthma camp?"

"Why are you excited to go back next year?"

Or the group of kids from the choir at our school, interviewed by one of the teachers who asked:

"What do you love about the school?"

"What's your favorite subject?"

"What do you want to be when you grow up?"

REHEARSING

The quality of the delivery of the Testimonial Speakers can make or break your program. I have seen a sixty-second testimonial from a teenage mother move a room of 600 people to tears, and I have also seen equally dedicated program recipients drone on or become overly emotional, only to lose the attention of the audience. Scripting and rehearsing your Testimonial Speakers is essential. Tell them they must follow the script and remind them that the program follows a tight timeline. Although there are no guarantees that the person will actually stick to the script, several practice runs of their testimonial, ideally in the same room where the Ask Event will take place, at the same microphone or podium, will put the speaker at ease and give you an opportunity to coach their speaking style and delivery.

CARING FOR YOUR SPEAKERS

You will need to assign at least one person to look after your Testimonial Speakers at the event—they will undoubtedly be nervous when they arrive. This "caretaker" person should call them (or their parents!) about a week before the event to confirm the schedule for the day, and then to reconfirm the day before. If the speaker is coming on their own, it often helps to offer to pick the person up and drive them to the event, to reassure them and make them feel more welcome—and to be sure they get there! If they do arrive alone, be sure to plan in advance where you will meet them and give them an emergency number for reaching you.

Invite your Testimonial Speakers to bring friends or family members if they would like. This will be a big day in their lives and they will want to share it. Arrange space for their guests to sit at a table with (or near) them. Be certain that your speakers get something to eat. Often in the nervous excitement, they will have neglected to do that. Bring an extra copy of their speech with you, just in case they have forgotten theirs.

It is fine if your speakers become emotional during their talk—within reason. If they stumble over a few words and get choked up, people will know how sincere they are. If they break down altogether and lose their place, give them a few seconds to compose themselves and move on. This is unlikely to happen if they have rehearsed their remarks several times, although the impact of standing in front of a large room of people who are all listening attentively can have a significant emotional effect on any speaker.

The person looking after the Testimonial Speaker needs to be positioned where the speaker can see them for cues, including the rehearsed cue for "time to stop." And finally, this nurturing person needs to congratulate the speaker after they have finished and escort them back to their seat.

In the case of a group of Testimonial Speakers, you will need a group of escorts and an empty table (or back room full of good food, in the case of kids) for them to retreat to after their part of the program is complete.

WHAT IF...?

Finally, what if your sole Testimonial Speaker does not show up at all on the day of the Ask Event? This has happened before. Have a staff member who worked closely with that person be prepared to read the same script the Testimonial Speaker was going to deliver. While it won't have quite the same impact, it is surprising how much emotion will come through because it is being read by someone well-acquainted with the person.

CHAPTER 15

THE PITCH

Now we are ready to talk about the final program element: the Pitch. Every bit of your hard work to put on the Ask Event culminates in the Pitch. Remember, there is no strong-arming necessary here. In the Raising More Money Model, asking for money should be nothing more than "nudging the inevitable." By now, the mix of compelling program elements will have done the job of ripening the fruit. The name and rationale for each of the Units of Service will be familiar to your guests. For example, they will have heard about your need to serve more campers or offer a whole new session of camp during the Visionary Leader Talk and in the video. At this point, people will either be ready to give, or not. There is no need to convince them of anything.

The job of the Pitch Person at the Ask Event is to focus on the people ready to give—to walk them through the pledge card line by line and help them fill out the form to make their gift that day. The Pitch Person has another critical role, especially at the first Ask Event: to introduce guests to the Multiple-Year Giving Society and tell them what each level of gift would provide for the work of the organization. Finally, the Pitch Person serves as a bit of a traffic cop, directing the flow of pledge cards and envelopes from the Table Captains to the guests and back to the Table Captains again. All of this is set out clearly in the pitch script and done with authentic appreciation for the generosity of the guests.

CHOOSING THE IDEAL PITCH PERSON

For your Pitch Person to qualify as a "credible school teacher-like" person, they must be truly tied to the mission, with a direct personal connection to the work of the organization, and they must be willing to follow a script. This person understands that their job is to walk people through the pledge card and help them give, and that this is a very specific and critical job. They are not trying to be a slick salesperson or an entertaining or motivational speaker. They are there because they truly love your organization and would love nothing more than for everyone in the audience to become part of the Multiple-Year Giving Society.

Do not assume that you need a big-name person in your community to be your Pitch Person. In fact, the ideal Pitch Person may be more of a "regular" person than a superstar. A parent or other family member who is a good public speaker can be an excellent Pitch Person. A longstanding, dedicated board member is often ideal. So long as they are truly passionate about your mission, will not deviate from the script, and are comfortable speaking in front of an audience, you will have made a good choice.

SCRIPT FOR THE PITCH

You do not want your guests to feel pressured in any way by the Pitch. You are not trying to push or prod them to do anything. Rather, they should feel wonderful about making their gift—it should be something they *want* to do, a natural expression of their commitment to your work. They should actually feel as if your organization is doing *their* work.

This fundraising model is about building lifelong relationships with donors who understand and value the work of your organization. We recognize and honor the natural "fruit ripening" process which cannot be rushed. I consider it a real testament to the model that only 40-50% of the guests make a contribution on the day of the event, because this shows that the others do not feel pressured to give at all. In fact, there is a piece built into the pitch script thanking everyone for coming and being part of this event, whether they have made a gift or not.

The following is a sample script for the Pitch:

SAMPLE PITCH SCRIPT

FREE ONE-HOUR ASK EVENT

Thanks to both of you for those great stories!

Hi, I'm *(your name)*, and I'd like to add my welcome and thanks to all of you for being here with us today. I'm fortunate to have been involved with *(name of organization)* for ten years, first by spending a year as a mentor, and now as Treasurer of the Board. I love this program because I have seen firsthand that it really has made a difference to many, many kids. As you've just heard, the kids love this organization too. And the mentors love it—being a senior friend remains to this day the best and most rewarding volunteer experience I've ever had. And it's a continuing privilege for me to support _____ and her wonderful staff in the great work that they do year after year.

When you came here today, most of you did not know exactly what we were going to ask you for in terms of your financial support. You probably came today because a friend invited you or because you already are familiar with our organization. But now that you've heard the full *(name of organization)* story and met some of our wonderful people, it's my privilege to ask you to make a financial investment in our ongoing success. This is not just an investment in *(name of organization)*; it truly is an investment in our own futures, and I believe that it is one of the most important investments that any of us can make.

When we looked at what we wanted to ask you for, we decided to request what we really need most—financial support for our day-to-day operations. There are thousands of children right here in this incredibly successful community who need the support of a positive mentor in their lives in order to reach their full potential. Your support can help ensure that we can reach these kids well into the future.

To build a stronger foundation for expanding our programs and to provide a stable future for *(name of organization)*, today we are launching a brand-new partnership—the Dream Builder Society. If you have been inspired by what you've seen today, I ask you now to consider joining me this morning as a founding member of our Society.

Now, I'd like to ask the Table Captains to pass out the pledge cards.

PAUSE ONLY BRIEFLY

Starting at the top of the card, the Dream Builder pledge level names are meant to give you a sense of what your contribution can do. Your contribution will go toward the unrestricted operating funds of *(name of organization)*.

1. The first giving level in the Dream Builder Society is a pledge of $1,000 each year for five years. We call this our "Building Hope" level because $1,000 is approximately the initial cost of finding and matching one mentor with one youth-in-need. So if you would consider a gift at this level, which is an average of just $83 per month, your gift would let us provide mentoring help to one new child for each of the next five years.

SAMPLE PITCH SCRIPT
CONTINUED

2. The next giving level in the Dream Builder Society is $10,000 a year for five years. This is our "Creating Dreams" level. If you would consider a gift of $10,000 each year for five years, you would allow us to match even more kids, plus support the friendships that graduate from our program as they continue their relationship into future years, as so many have.

3. We know that many of you are part of a company or foundation, or you may just be in a position to give more. So the next level is "Changing Lives," which lets you have a far-ranging impact on the lives of youth in our community. If you would consider a gift of $25,000 a year for five years, that would be a major boost to expanding our geographic and program reach—providing weekly relationship-building support, recreational activities, life-skills workshops, academic support, and career-building activities to youth-in-need throughout our area.

If you are joining me today as a founding member of the Dream Builder Society, my personal thanks for your generous support!

Although I started by introducing the Dream Builder Society, we know and respect that you may prefer to give at a different level, and so we provide the next line just for you. On this line, please tell us how much you would like to give and for how many years.

We truly appreciate whatever level of support you can provide and we ask that you make the first payment on your pledge today.

Perhaps you would like to consider a gift of stock or something else. Or, you simply have some great ideas for us. If so, please check the next box, the one that says, "Please contact me, I have other thoughts to share."

I know that many of you are still writing, but, if I could have your attention here for just a moment, it's important that you really hear what I'm about to say. Whatever gift you have chosen to make today—whether you have become a founding member of our Dream Builder Society, made a gift at a different level, or have ideas that you want to share with us later, we sincerely thank each and every one of you on behalf of the great kids we serve. And we thank you all for the most important gift you gave today, the gift of your valuable time. We really appreciate that you took time out of your busy lives to be here this morning to learn more about *(name of organization)*.

I'll give you some time now to finish filling out the cards; when you are finished, please pass your envelopes back to your Table Captain.

Now, I'll turn the program back to _____ to wrap up.

SAMPLE PLEDGE CARD WORDING

FREE ONE-HOUR ASK EVENT

(ORGANIZATION NAME) CAN COUNT ON MY SUPPORT

I would like to become a founding member of the Dream Builder Society:

___ Sponsor a Student: $1,000 per year for 5 years

___ Sponsor Ten Students: $10,000 per year for 5 years

___ Sponsor a Classroom: $25,000 per year for 5 years

I would like to contribute in other ways:

___ Contribute $_____for_____years.

___ Please contact me. I have other thoughts to share.

_____

PAYMENT:

_____ My check is enclosed, made payable to: _____

_____ Please charge my Visa/MC#_____Exp._____

_____ Please contact me about paying my pledge with stock.

_____ My company will match my gift.

We will bill you in (*month*) for your annual pledge unless you request

otherwise_____

_____

Date _____

Name _____

Organization _____

Address _____

City _____ State _____ Zip _____

Day Phone _____ Evening Phone _____

E-mail Address _____

For more sample pitch scripts and pledge cards used by Raising More Money alumni organizations, see pages 197 and 209 in the Samples.

EVENT AFTERMATH:
SUSTAINING THE CYCLE

CHAPTER 16

CELEBRATING YOUR
ASK EVENT RESULTS

Suddenly, just like a wonderful party you have worked for months to prepare, the Ask Event is over in a flash. The room has emptied out, the lingering board members and volunteers have left, and there you are, in a state of exhaustion, shock, and euphoria. The first tendency will be to review all that went wrong—the glitch with the audio/visual equipment or the lights, the Testimonial Speaker who spoke too long, the coffee that wasn't hot enough.

Resist the temptation to do the post-mortem until you have counted the money. I will never forget the way I felt after our first Ask Event at the inner-city Seattle academy where the model was developed. After the whole crowd had left, I found myself alone in the ballroom with the board chair and my husband. They reassured me that the event had been a brilliant success, but I did not believe them. Our team had been up all night setting up the room for 1,000 people (we weren't able to get into the room until the banquet from the previous night had ended). Although our event had started and ended on time, so many elements of the program had not gone as planned that all I could rehash in my mind were the glaring mistakes. I was certain the event had been a huge failure.

Finally my husband looked me in the eyes and said, "Honey, go count the money!" I knew I had to do that, frightened as I was. We had arranged a little room next to the ballroom where the rest of the team was waiting with an old-style adding machine with a paper tape. They had all the pledge envelopes stacked in a pile, but they were waiting for me to open them, one by one, so we could do the accounting together.

Out of the 850 people who attended that first event, 115 of them had pledged $1,000 a year for each of the next five years. We were absolutely stunned. Another eight had pledged $10,000 a year for the next five years, and four more people had given at the highest level we had asked for: $25,000 a year for each of the next five years. As I write this, I still am in awe of people's extraordinary generosity when presented with the facts and emotional appeal of an organization in such a straightforward way.

True to what I now know to be the formula, only about 50% of the guests gave anything at all that day. Of those who did not give, many left notes on their pledge cards saying they needed to talk to someone else about making a larger gift to the school. Many had foundations or corporations that needed to process checks in a more formal way. The money poured in for several months after the event.

There were two big lessons I learned that day, one good, one quite painful. The first is that event organizers are not the best judges of the event's success. The organizers will naturally dwell on what went wrong. But the guests did not know how it was *supposed* to go; they only have their experience of how it went. If you follow this model closely, your event will seem highly professional and uniquely forthright, even if it is hard for you, as the organizer, to see that. People will be talking about it for days to come.

The painful lesson I learned was to prepare in advance for the job of entering all the data accurately. I presumed that a clerical person would be able to enter all the gift data in the days following the event. After all, we had already entered the names and contact information of most of the guests based on the lists the Table Captains had submitted prior to the event. Upon closer inspection of the pledge cards, I realized that, in spite of our best efforts to make the pledge card simple and clear, it was still hard to tell how each donor wanted to be named, and, in some cases, how much they had intended to give. I had to phone many of the donors to clarify information (which was, of course, the perfect opportunity to thank them). I took back the data entry job and personally entered each gift and pledge, which to this day has fueled my passion for having an outstanding donor and volunteer tracking system that everyone on the team can use.

In the hours following the event, treat yourself to the hard-earned satisfaction of opening the envelopes. Get out the adding machine and, as they say, "do the math"!

By the time we tallied everything up and drove back to the office, the phone was blinking away with nearly 100 messages, people calling to congratulate us and to say it was the single best "fundraising event" they had ever attended. People had so many more ideas for us, names of people they wished had been included, people they wanted to have come to Point of Entry Events right away. In short, people's natural propensity for contribution had been unleashed by the power of the event. There was no stopping them. I knew we needed to get in gear with the follow-up right away.

CHAPTER 17

POST-EVENT FOLLOW-UP: ASSESSING YOUR ASK EVENT'S STRENGTHS AND WEAKNESSES

Regardless of the financial results of your first Ask Event, you no doubt generated tremendous interest and goodwill towards your organization. The single most common statement we hear from groups after their Ask Events, whether they raise several million or several thousand, is: "It was about *so much more* than the money." The second most frequent comment is: "Now we see all the ways to make the event better next year."

While the details of the event are still fresh in your mind, debrief each aspect of the event with your core team and assess what you would do differently next time.

At Raising More Money, we closely monitor the Ask Events of the organizations that go through our Raising More Money Workshops and analyze their success, one by one. While most of our groups meet or exceed their financial goals for their Ask Events, those that fall short have usually deviated from the model in one or more ways. The event organizers are often not the best judges of where the event might have fallen short. For example, they may feel that the video was sufficiently emotional or that the Testimonial Speakers were effective, whereas honest feedback from some of the guests might tell them otherwise.

When I made my Follow-Up Calls after the first event, I remember the most common complaint was about the food. It would never have occurred to me to consider that a problem because I was so nervous at the event, I didn't eat a thing. Had I not asked for feed-back from the guests, I never would have known. So be sure to do some informal polling rather than presuming that you know how your guests experienced the event.

If your event fell short of your goals, or if you just want even better results next time, take care and consider during the Follow-Up process whether you avoided each of these pitfalls.

ASK EVENT PITFALLS
Not enough emotion in the program

- What was the opening Emotional Hook in the program?
- Did the opening Emotional Hook relate to the mission?
- Did the opening Emotional Hook involve the people served by the organization or relate to their issues and needs?
- Was there enough music in the program?
- Did the Visionary Leader tell stories about the work of the organization or share their personal reasons for being involved?
- Did each person on the program convey their genuine connection to the organization's mission?
- Did the video touch people and move them to tears three times?
- Were the Testimonial Speakers moving?
- Did the real impact of your organization's work come through as the Testimonial Speakers told their stories?

"Creativity" with the giving levels on the pledge card

- Did the pledge card clearly list the levels of the Multiple-Year Giving Society?
- Did you have only the three recommended levels?
  Was the lowest level $1,000 a year?
- Were the three levels either: $1,000, $5,000, and $10,000 or $1,000, $10,000, and $25,000?
- Were all of the levels clearly listed as a multiple-year pledge for five years?

- Did the names of the levels make sense and fit together logically? (e.g., Sponsor a Camper, Sponsor a Cabin, Sponsor a Camp)
- Were the needs for each of these three "items" referenced throughout the program? (e.g., "We turn away 100 kids each year who want to come to camp.")

The Pitch Person didn't follow the script

- Did the Pitch Person understand the Raising More Money Model?
- Did the Pitch Person understand the Multiple-Year Giving Society?
- Did the Pitch Person have a written, prepared script based on the Raising More Money script?
- Did the Pitch Person rehearse the script in advance with others who gave honest feedback?
- Did the Pitch Person actually follow the script on the day of the event?
- Did the Pitch Person walk the guests through each line of the pledge card according to the script?
- Did the Pitch Person pause long enough to give the guests time to fill out the cards?
- Did the Pitch Person ask the guests to pass their pledge cards to their Table Captains when they were finished filling them out?

Guests were not properly prepared

- Had at least 20% of the guests at the Ask Event attended a Point of Entry Event within the last year?
- Was each guest invited word-of-mouth by a friend who followed the explicit invitation wording, making clear that they would be asked to give money at the event but also that giving was not required?

- Had someone from the organization personally invited all key supporters of the organization, such as current and former board members, donors, and dedicated volunteers?

Deviating from the rules about Table Captains

- Were the 15% attrition rates for Table Captains and their guests factored into the initial projections?
- Were less than 10% of the Table Captains staff members?
- Did each Table Captain attend a Point of Entry prior to the Ask Event?
- Were the remaining Table Captains chosen for their passion, or merely because they were obliged to be Table Captains? (for example, because they were on the board)
- Were all Table Captains briefed on their roles before and during the event, including the specific wording for inviting their guests to sit at their table?
- Did Table Captains have at least 20% of their guests attend a Point of Entry Event prior to the Ask Event?
- Did each Table Captain fill out a pledge card at the same time as the rest of the guests?

Not sticking to the timeline or the program for the event

- Did the program start and end on time?
- Was the meal pre-set with no serving people distracting guests' attention from the program?
- Did any of the program elements run particularly longer than expected?
- Did you include any program elements other than those outlined in the model? For example: an awards presentation, keynote speaker, or anything else that might have detracted from 100% focus on the mission?

FOLLOW-UP CALLS

The two-week period after the Ask Event is, by far, the most fertile time for additional fundraising as well as cultivation of your new Multiple-Year Donors. This is not the time for the event organizers to go on vacation! While you may be tired and ready for a break, your guests, on the other hand, have just gotten interested. Now is the time they are curious and eager to learn more. This post-event follow-up can be the most exciting and productive part of the process. If you have followed our road map until now, and especially if there was enough emotion present in your event program, there will be much more ripened fruit to be picked in these critical weeks. The Follow-Up Calls after the Ask Event are structured much like the calls that follow the Point of Entry (see page 6). By following these steps precisely, many groups have more than doubled their total results.

THE FIVE-STEP FOLLOW-UP CALL

1. Thank you for coming.

2. What did you think?

3. Be quiet and listen.

4. Is there any way you could see yourself becoming involved with us?

5. Is there anyone else you can think of that we ought to invite to a _____ (Point of Entry)?

WHO MAKES THE FOLLOW-UP CALLS

The calls should be made by a high-level core group of two or three "insiders" who attended the Ask Event. These are people who are senior enough in the organization so that their calls really mean something to the people receiving the calls. Their main role will be to thank people and to listen well for the cues about how that person wants to be cultivated.

MANAGING THE FOLLOW-UP CALL DATA

Establish a system for the follow-up, to make sure that all information (referrals, ideas, etc.) ends up in your central database. Many organizations create a Follow-Up Call form or template that team members can complete after each contact with a donor or potential interested party. If you are using our Raising More Money Next Step online software, these forms are built into the system and can be completed and submitted online, or they may be turned in by fax or e-mail to the person accountable for the Raising More Money process.

WHO MUST BE CALLED

All Table Captains

Call all Table Captains within twenty-four hours. (For a breakfast event, call on the same day.) Use the five-step Follow-Up Call process, modified as follows.

Thank the Table Captain. It was their hard work that filled the event and ultimately made it so successful.

Ask your Table Captains: "What did you think of the event? What did you hear from your guests?" You are listening for comments about guests who took their pledge card with them and told their Table Captain, "I have to discuss this with someone else, but I really want to support this organization." When you hear these comments, add these people to your personal phone call follow-up list.

Encourage your Table Captains to call all of their guests to thank them for attending. A voicemail message from the Table Captains to their guests is fine, just be sure the Table Captains know not to ask their guests for money in this call.

If the Table Captains are very excited about how the event went, ask: "Is there any other way you would like to become more involved with us? Is there any other way you would like to participate?" Listen closely to their responses. Also ask: "Would you like to be a Table Captain again next year?"

Then, ask: "Is there anyone else you can think of that we ought to invite to a _____ (Point of Entry)?" Suggest that they invite those people to a Point of Entry Event between now and next year. If, for some reason, they themselves have not attended a Point of Entry Event, invite them to do so. Tell them that their feedback about the Point of Entry would be very helpful, and tell them when the next one is scheduled to take place.

All Multiple-Year Donors

The day of or the day following the event, start calling all Multiple-Year Donors. Customize the five-step Follow-Up Call process as follows.

Thank them sincerely for their contribution. Make them feel special for joining the Multiple-Year Giving Society and taking a leadership role.

Ask: "What did you think of the event?" Listen closely to their responses. If they have any specific concerns (about the food, the venue, the program), acknowledge those concerns and thank them for their honest feedback.

If the donors are very excited about the work of the organization, ask if they would like to become more involved. Is there any other way they would like to participate? Listen closely to their responses. Also ask if they would like to be a Table Captain next year.

Ask: "Is there anyone else you can think of that we ought to invite to a _____ (Point of Entry)?" Suggest that they invite those people to a Point of Entry Event between now and next year. If they themselves have not attended a Point of Entry Event, invite them to do so. Tell them that their feedback about the Point of Entry would be very helpful, and tell them when the next one is scheduled to take place.

If you have an upcoming Free Feel-Good Cultivation Event scheduled for large donors, tell them a little bit about it to pique their interest and ask them to save the date.

"Thoughts to Share" People

Next, contact the people who indicated "I have other thoughts to share" on their pledge card. Thank them for coming, and ask: "What are your thoughts? What ideas do you have?" During this time, listen and take notes. Then thank them for their ideas and suggestions, and let them know what your next steps will be.

If they are very excited about the work of the organization, ask if they would like to become more involved. Is there any other way they would like to participate? Listen closely to their responses. Also ask if they would like to be a Table Captain next year.

Ask: "Is there anyone else you can think of that we ought to invite to a _____ (Point of Entry)?" Suggest that they invite those people to a Point of Entry Event between now and next year. If they themselves have not attended a Point of Entry Event, invite them to do so. Tell them that their feedback about the Point of Entry would be very helpful, and tell them when the next one is scheduled to take place.

All Other Donors

Contact all other donors. Decide on a "cut-off" dollar amount, and call the higher-level donors. Use these same modified Follow-Up Call steps.

Thank them for coming and giving what they gave. Ask: "What did you think of the event?" Listen for feedback, ideas.

If they are very excited about the work of the organization, ask if they would like to become more involved. Is there any other way they would like to participate? Listen closely to their responses. Also ask if they would like to be a Table Captain next year.

Ask: "Is there anyone else you can think of that we ought to invite to a _____ (Point of Entry)?" Suggest that they invite that person to a Point of Entry Event between now and next year. If they themselves have not attended a Point of Entry Event, invite them to do so. Tell them that their feedback about the Point of Entry would be very helpful, and tell them when the next one is scheduled to take place.

No-Shows

Contact all those people who were expected at the Ask Event but did not come. You will know who these people are because their nametags will have been left on the nametag table at the Ask Event. Divide your list into two groups.

First, contact donors and friends of the organization who have already been well cultivated and are ready to be asked, but were unable to attend the event. Call each of these people and say: "We missed you at the event; here are some of the highlights from the event." You can then include quotes from the Visionary Leader speech or offer to send a copy of the video to the people on this list. "We launched the Multiple-Year Giving Society to ensure the financial strength of our organization and the sustainability of our work in the community." Invite them to a Point of Entry or a one-on-one meeting where, if appropriate, you can consider asking them to give.

Second, contact people you do not know at all, for whom the Ask Event would have been a Point of Entry. These names should be collected and reviewed at a subsequent board, staff, or volunteer meeting to determine who has connections with these people and could call and invite them to a Point of Entry.

Those Who Did Not Give

Follow up by mail with those people who attended the Ask Event but did not give. You do not have permission to call them. However, these people are still on your Cultivation Superhighway. Just because they did not give at the event does not mean that they aren't interested in your organization. Remember, the Ask Event was a mini-Point of Entry for many people. Now you need to take steps to find out how to cultivate these people—with their permission— so that they might become volunteers or donors later.

Send a letter to thank these guests for attending the event. Tell them you really appreciate their support, and hope they found the event informative and inspiring. Invite them to attend a Point of Entry and include dates of upcoming Point of Entry Events and instructions on how to RSVP. If you do not hear back from them, "bless and release" them. Do not add them to your direct mail list.

Critically assessing your Ask Event's strengths and weaknesses in this way and rigorously implementing this detailed follow-up strategy will enhance your success each year.

Next, before we discuss how to take care of your new donors, let's talk about how to ask one-on-one.

CHAPTER 18

ONE-ON-ONE ASKING

$\mathbf{A}$s you recall, the Ask Event is only one of the two ways of asking for money in this model. The second way is to ask one-on-one in-person. For many groups we work with, this is the preferred method of asking. Most groups ask both ways. Over time, as the model becomes more of a bridge strategy into major gifts, capital campaigns, endowments, and planned giving, one-on-one asking will become the predominant mode of asking. It is a good idea to get started with one-on-one asking as soon as you begin implementing the model.

DECIDING WHO TO ASK ONE-ON-ONE

The first people to ask one-on-one are the larger potential do-nors who also have been well-cultivated and are strong contenders for making a leadership or Challenge Gift or for sponsoring the costs of the event. In this case, you will want to ask these people for their gifts before your Ask Event so you will be able to announce their gift at the event. Even if these donors prefer not to be identified at the Ask Event, their gifts will make an enormous difference in leveraging others and will go a long way toward making or exceeding your over-all goal for the event. These Asks are generally for the largest level of your Multiple-Year Giving Society, often $25,000 a year (or more) for each of the next five years. In some cases, these will be one-year gifts as opposed to five-year pledges.

Second are the people who have attended your Point of Entry Events, been followed up with, and have gotten involved with the organization. Yet, for whatever reason, they are unable to attend the Ask Event. In some cases, you will know this in advance. In other cases, they will have a last-minute emergency which prevents them from coming to the event. In either case, I recommend waiting until after the Ask Event to meet with them and ask them for a contribution. This is because it will be far more natural to meet with them to share your excitement about the event, explain the launching of the Multiple-Year Giving Society and the various giving levels, and invite them to become part of this giving society.

Third are donors who attended an Ask Event where the Pitch failed to engender many gifts, for whatever reason. If there was enough emotion in the event program and the guests were truly inspired, many of the Asks can be done afterwards, even by telephone. This is only an emergency strategy; it is extremely labor intensive, yet it will work in a pinch.

WHO SHOULD ASK?

We refer to these as "one-on-one" Asks, but in reality there are generally two people asking one potential donor or donor couple. Ideally, the askers will be one staff person and one board member or volunteer who know the donor and have been involved in the cultivation process. Both askers should be prepared to "pop the question" depending on what feels natural at that moment.

The Ask generally takes place during a scheduled appointment with the donor, either at the organization's offices or at a place convenient to the donor, such as the donor's office or home. Just as with the "ripened fruit" donors at the Ask Event, these one-on-one Ask donors should be well cultivated and predisposed to give before the Ask. This Ask should not come as a surprise to anyone. The donor should be giving you signs and cues that they are ready to give. If it still feels premature to be asking this person for money, the best thing to do is to have another cultivation contact—such as a visit to your program to talk with the staff person or participants involved with the program they most love—before you ask. Trust your instincts, and remember this is about treating the donor the way you would want to be treated: with respect and dignity. Know that this is a person who is passionate about your mission, and, in the Ask meeting, do not relate to this person as if they are a distant stranger. Treat this person as if they were a lifelong personal friend. Do not push them to give more than they will feel good about. You want to keep the door open for the future. Leave the donor in the driver's seat, always.

Having said that, you should definitely have a suggested dollar amount in mind when you ask. Also, remember to include an emotional story and reference the work of the organization. You are asking for funding for your work, not for you personally. Talk about the difference this gift will make for the organization.

ASKING BOARD MEMBERS TO GIVE

Asking board members to give is often a sensitive topic. In the Raising More Money Model, giving money personally is one of the three prescribed roles for board members (the others are inviting people to Point of Entry Events and making thank-you calls to happy donors). However, we do not recommend a minimum gift size for all board members. If you shift your mindset to treat your board members as if they were your most cherished major donors, they soon will find themselves giving very naturally.

Therefore, unless you are planning to ask your board members for leadership or Challenge Gifts, it is fine to include your board in the normal asking process which will take place at the Ask Event. And, just like many of your other donors, these board members will often find themselves giving more at the event than they might otherwise give.

Those board members who are unable to attend the event should be asked one-on-one after the event. Use the same pledge card and levels you launched at the Ask Event.

"COUNTING" THIS MONEY
TOWARDS THE EVENT

All the money that is raised surrounding the Ask Event through these one-on-one Asks may be "counted" towards the results of your Ask Event. Just like the people who take home their pledge cards from the event and mail them in later, these people you ask personally within a month or two before or after the event can count towards your total. After all, the momentum of the event is the catalyst for the Ask.

Let's move on to look at how to take care of your new donors.

CHAPTER 19

TAKING CARE OF YOUR
NEW DONORS

After putting on their first successful Ask Event as well as many one-on-one Asks, most groups find themselves in unfamiliar territory, asking, "What do we do now with all these new Multiple-Year Donors?"

This chapter will give you a template for donor appreciation, recognition, cultivation, and pledge collection that works beautifully—if you follow it.

STRATIFY YOUR NEW DONORS

The first thing to do is divide your new donors by giving level. Start with each of your Units of Service—for example, $25,000 a year for five years, $10,000 a year for five years, and $1,000 a year for five years. The next level will be donors of $500-$999, then donors of $250-$499, donors of $100-$249, and then everyone who gave less than $100.

Over the next year, each of these groups will receive different forms of recognition and communication, beginning with their first official thank-you letter (required by the Internal Revenue Service in the United States). This letter should be sent within two weeks of the Ask Event to every single donor.

I recommend that each of these thank-you letters be signed personally by the executive director or board chair. Letters to donors of $1,000 or more should also contain a personal note from the same signer, such as "thanks for your support," "thank you for your generous gift," or "it was great to see you"; something that shows the donor that a real person at the organization knows that they gave.

In addition to the first official thank-you letter, your new Multiple-Year Donors will receive another personal form of recognition. At our school, each donor of $1,000 a year for five years received a drawing from a child in a colored cardboard frame. It said a big "Thank You" at the bottom, in the child's writing, and was signed with the child's first name and the name of the school. Very simple and very personal.

The Multiple-Year Donors of $10,000 and $25,000 each received an eight-foot-long scroll of butcher paper with hand-prints and "thank you's" drawn in crayon. At the bottom, it said: "Thank you from Mrs. Johnson's second grade class." These scrolls were delivered to each donor personally, at their workplace if possible, by the principal and a group of the kids. It took a little effort to coordinate these "secret" visits, but the impact on the donors (and their co-workers) was remarkable. People treasure these simple gifts and, most of all, they can't help but realize that you truly do appreciate them for giving.

While this level of personal attention may seem time consuming and excessive, you need to get used to it. This is the new reality of personalized recognition and appreciation that begins the process of having your organization stand out in the minds of your new donors and reaffirms that they gave to a great group. Beyond that, of course, it sets the tone for ongoing personal cultivation and contact, stratified by giving level, with each donor.

One final word about direct mail. People often ask if they should continue to send their annual fundraising mailings to their new Multiple-Year Donors. Our rule is that once a donor pledges $1,000 or more for five years, their name should be removed from your direct mail list and, as much as possible, all subsequent contacts should be in-person.

PLEDGE COLLECTION

Your pledge collection rate for the pledges of $1,000 and higher should be over 95%. This is because you will be in contact with your Multiple-Year Donors many times over the course of each year. In fact, many people may send in their pledge payment naturally in the course of the year. Therefore, pledge collection need not be a tense waiting game. Your pledge card includes a note telling people that you will invoice them at the same time every year, so they should be expecting to receive it. Think of this invoice as one more contact on the Cultivation Superhighway in your lifelong relationship with this donor. Most people appreciate that reminder. If they do not respond within one month of the invoice, call them to check in and ask if there is anything else they need. If necessary, send a second reminder a month later.

THE SCIENCE OF "SPECIAL"

Before we talk about turning all of this into an ongoing system, let's recall why we are doing all of this in the first place. What we are working to develop and cultivate are lifelong donors, donors who care deeply about the mission of the organization and choose to stay involved for the long term. Over time, many of these donors will become major donors, giving to capital and endowment, and ultimately allowing your organization's private funding to become self-sustaining.

Take a minute to think about your lifelong friends and family. For better or worse, you have a dialog with them, a give-and-take with talking and listening back and forth. That is what keeps the relationship alive. That is what lets those people know they matter to you. It tells them that they are special.

What if we could dissect those dialogs a bit further? What if you could have that same sort of dialog with your donors and then turn it into a system that could be tracked and managed ongoingly, long after you are gone from the organization? That is what we mean by the science of "special," and it is the essence of every contact on the Cultivation Superhighway.

CONTACTS ON THE CULTIVATION SUPERHIGHWAY

The purpose of each contact is to deepen your involvement and connection with that donor, continuing to ripen the fruit. People often ask, "how many contacts do we need before we can ask for money?" There is no "right" answer to that question. It varies according to the donor. If you view the cultivation process as ongoing for life, each "next Ask" would be nothing more than another natural contact at the perfect moment when the fruit is ripened. Instead of an ordeal to be dreaded, each Ask should be a natural harvesting of the ripened fruit.

There is no place in this model for random or superficial contacts initiated by the organization. This should relieve you of a great deal of time-consuming mailing and party planning and allow you to focus on having a more customized dialog with each of your individual donors.

To create that customized dialog, each contact must be personal, according to our specific definition of the word. For a contact to qualify as personal in the Raising More Money Model, it needs to meet all five of these criteria.

THE DEFINITION OF PERSONAL

One-on-one, speaking only to them, making each donor feel special

It can't feel generic. It can't feel so standard and impersonal that the donor knows that this identical contact is being made with every other donor (even though that may be the case). Each communication has got to be customized enough that the donor feels that you are speaking only to them and you know what they need to feel special.

Face-to-face, by phone, or e-mail

Be sure the donor can respond right in the process of the contact. The medium matters. There is no substitute for in-person, face-to-face communication. It allows for the immediate give-and-take we are looking for in a true dialog. It lets you have eye contact, read body cues, and shake hands. The telephone offers another medium for dialog, letting you pick up voice inflection, pauses, hesitations, and subtle levels of interest. We also include e-mail in our definition of personal. It allows for dialog and can be extremely personal if directed to each person individually. We include in this category only the type of personal e-mails you might send to family members or friends, not blanket group e-mails.

Relevant to the donor's self-interest

Focus each contact on whatever aspect of your program or service interests your donor most. For example, a health research organization could invite the donor to meet individually or in a group of donors with a research scientist who is working on the disease they have expressed a particular interest in. You will get to know your larger donors well enough to anticipate their preferences and interests.

Timed to the donor's pace

Each of us operates at our own pace, some faster, some slower. Thinking again of your friends and family, you know whose e-mails or phone calls you must reply to right away, versus those you can take a little longer to get back to. The same is true of your donors. Start with a one-week response time, at the longest, to each donor communication. As you learn each donor's unique pace, you can adjust this to be faster or slower.

Delivered via the donor's preferred medium

This is very important in our world of rapid communication and personalization. Think of the many ways you have of communicating with your friends and family. You know how each person prefers to be communicated with. Think of which medium they use to connect with you. It may be more than one. Is it via phone or voicemail, fax, e-mail, or in-person?

A WORD ABOUT HAND-WRITTEN LETTERS

People often express concern that this model no longer values the personal hand-written note or letter. They cite examples of letters people keep over the years as compared to short-lived e-mail or voice conversations. They ask if there is a place for these letters in our model.

Certainly, if you know your donor prefers to receive hand-written letters, keep sending them. To incorporate them into our model, add a line to the letter that invites feedback or suggests that you will be calling the person in the next few days to get their thoughts on something mentioned in the letter. That will allow for the permission-based dialog essential to the model.

PERSONALIZING YOUR CONTACTS

Let's look at how your organization is currently contacting your donors and how you could simultaneously streamline that process and allow for more customization.

Take a look at this sample chart tracking Personalized Contacts on the Cultivation Superhighway.

PERSONALIZED CONTACTS ON THE CULTIVATION SUPERHIGHWAY

	LEAST PERSONAL	MORE PERSONAL	MOST PERSONAL	NEXT ACTION
	• Printed • Generic/same for all • By mail or bulk mail	• Hand-written note • Sent 1st class mail • Fax	• Phone • E-mail • In person • Multiple people contact the person (with permission) • From high-level person	What we will do to move to "Most Personal"
INFORM				
INVITE				
ASK				
THANK				

Down the left of the chart are the four main reasons we have for staying in contact with our donors and potential donors: to *inform* them, to *invite* them, to *ask* them, and to *thank* them. Across the top are three increasing levels of personal contact, with examples of how to "warm up" the contact a little more at each level. For example, right now, what is a simple example of the "Least Personal" way your organization informs people on a regular basis about your work? Perhaps your standard monthly or quarterly newsletter, delivered via bulk mail, comes to mind.

Now, moving to the middle column, "More Personal," what could you do with that same impersonal quarterly newsletter to "warm it up" a bit? You could attach a special note highlighting an article that you know will be of interest to the person, and then mail it via first-class mail (not bulk mail) or e-mail or fax it to the person.

Moving over to the third "most personal" column, what could you do to warm it up even more? You could call the person and tell them that this special letter or fax or e-mail is coming, or you could arrange a meeting to show it to them or deliver it in-person. If you take time to read through the chart on page 150, you will see that adding contacts from multiple people (for example, a board member and a volunteer who is also a personal friend) can increase the customization and, in a very natural way, make the donor feel unique and special.

I highly recommend you do this exercise with your team. Draw out this grid and fill in the blanks with what you are currently doing. Then, in the fourth column, write in the "Next Actions" you can take to increase your level of personalization for each type of contact.

You will notice some interesting and reassuring things if you take the time to do this:

1. The least personal contacts may actually take more time for less return than the most personal contacts. For example, spending several days working on a bulk mailing for a newsletter may yield a lot less than spending that same time calling, e-mailing, or meeting with certain donors you know will have an interest in the programs highlighted in the newsletter.

2. The middle column, "More Personal," is no longer sufficient for building long-lasting relationships. It used to be that a printed invitation with a hand-written note on it would be sufficient to have people RSVP yes to an upcoming event. That is not the case today. I find I still ignore such invitations unless I receive more than one, each signed by a friend, letting me know how much they want me to attend, possibly also reinforced in a phone call or personal meeting.

3. The importance of "personal." In our incredibly busy world, where people are bombarded with all types of information, your communication has got to be really personal and customized to each of your donors in order to stand out.

This explains why, in the Raising More Money Model, the Ask Event is Table Captain-driven and why your Point of Entry Events will also be driven by personal invitations. To be successful with this fundraising approach, you will need to become comfortable with picking up the phone and calling someone personally or sending them personal e-mails, so that you treat them just as you would treat your lifelong friends and family members.

YOUR RECOGNITION AND CULTIVATION PLAN

Now let's look at how you can turn all this into a system. Rather than trying to second-guess your donors and then provide them with random appreciation and sporadic contacts, your organization is probably overdue for a well-thought-out system of recognition and cultivation. Also, as your base of donors, volunteers, and friends grows, it will be helpful to have a system for tracking when and how you formally contact them to deepen the cultivation process.

Recognition is a key component in your system of personalized cultivation. As with many other aspects of the Raising More Money Model, you are probably already doing a great deal to stay connected and say thank you. Yet without a recognition system that will live on beyond your tenure with your organization, your legacy will be incomplete and you will undermine your efforts to keep your donors for life.

Designing your recognition/cultivation system is relatively simple and can be fun. You will finally be able to give yourself credit for all the things you are doing right. The critical element in streamlining this process is to have all the key players in the room as you do it.

Start by identifying all the internal people who already have some part in the process. These will be people whose work connects you to your broader community—the data entry person, the people who plan your special events, the grant writers, the development committee, the staff who work with donors and volunteers, the folks in the accounting department, and the board members.

Assemble all these people (or at least one representative from each group) in one room where you have papered the walls with newsprint. Across the top, make twelve columns for the months of the year. Down the left side list all your constituent groups, broken down as specifically as possible—donors at various levels, volunteers in various programs, and clients or patrons in whatever categories you normally speak of.

Be sure to solicit input from each member of the team. Each of you is an expert in one particular piece of the puzzle. Then go back and fill in the boxes, month by month, with what you are already doing to recognize or connect with this group of people in that month.

For example, if you normally have a volunteer recognition dinner for your soup kitchen volunteers in May, put the name of that event in the proper box. Regular mailings, newsletters, and annual reports can be added into the appropriate months. Other special events throughout the year should be inserted in the box for the group they are targeted for. You may want to color code all the mailings in yellow, all the events in blue, all the times donors will be asked for money in green, etc.

CLARIFY WHO IS ACCOUNTABLE

Now go back and put the title (not the person's name) of the person accountable for making each of those things happen. If the personal hand-written holiday note to all donors over $5,000 is always written by the executive director, write that title in. If the invitation to the graduation ceremony is done by the parents' com-

SAMPLE ANNUAL RECOGNITION/CULTIVATION PLAN

Legend: ● In Person ◐ Mail ○ Fax ◑ Phone ◒ Online

Category	JANUARY	FEBRUARY	MARCH	APRIL	MAY	JUNE	JULY	AUGUST	SEPTEMBER	OCTOBER	NOVEMBER	DECEMBER
DONORS:												
Sponsor a Classroom ($25,000/yr x 5 years)	1 on 1 Lunch with E.D. and Board Chair				Classroom Sponsor Private Dinner			Board-Hosted Golf Day with Lunch		Classroom Sponsor Private Dinner	Telephone Follow-Up & Interviews	Asked to be Table Captains Next Year
Sponsor Ten Students ($10,000/yr x 5 years)	1 on 1 Follow-Up with their Request	Donor-Hosted Points of Entry or Re-Entry		Spring Field Day		Pre-Graduation Reception						Holiday Mailing to Non-Event Donors
Sponsor a Student ($1,000/yr x 5 years)	Thank You Calls from E.D./Board Chair	Post-Holiday Thankathon & Interviews; Invite to:	Annual Report Mailed									
$500 - $999												
$250 - $499												
$100 - $249												
<$100												
All Year:				E-mail and Fax Updates Monthly (All Year)					Back-to-School Open House/Curriculum Fair	Invite to Free One-Hour Ask Event	Free One-Hour Ask Event	
NEWSLETTER	(Jan)					(June)				(Oct)		
VOLUNTEERS												
Current Board	Board Planning Retreat	Board/E.D. 1 on 1 Interviews						Nominating Committee "Resup" Calls				Board Recognition Dinner
Past Board												
Current Committee Members												
Tutors			Thank You Calls from E.D.	1 on 1 Meetings with E.D. / Site Visit from E.D.								
Mentors	Site Visit from E.D.			Mentoring Program Dinner	Volunteer Recognition Luncheon	Graduation (Reserved Seats)	E.D. Site Visits / Special Summer Program	Summer Graduation		E.D. Site Visit		
Computer Program Volunteers			Computer Night									
Music Program Volunteers		Winter Concert										
STAFF												
Main Office		Administrative Staff Retreat										All Staff Holiday Party
Program Staff			Program Staff Retreat		Staff Picnic							Holiday Gifts to Staff
Satellite Youth Program Staff												

1 on 1 Notes and Birthday Cards from Supervisor (All Staff, All Year) mittee chairperson, write that title in.

Fill in everything you can think of. Then identify who else might be missing. You may realize that one of the satellite programs puts on some special educational evenings that you haven't been tracking. You had better call that person and have them look over your chart to give their input.

Next, as a team, stand back from the chart and notice where there are empty boxes. Has a donor at the $500 to $999 level not had contact from you for four months in a row? What would be a legitimate contact you could add in just the right month? Perhaps it would be a thank-you call from a board member or a key volunteer.

Then go back through the chart, looking at the categories of people you have listed down the left-hand side. Take them one at a time and walk through the flow of the year from the perspective of those in that category. Does it make sense that they are receiving invitations and letters from three different people in the same month? Have you removed them from the direct mail program once they begin giving at a certain level? Where in the annual cycle is the opportunity for each group listed to give feedback about how you are doing? Is there enough real-person contact, or is too much done via the mail? What other information are you missing? Flesh out your chart with the kind of rich detail you want future generations to know about.

ZOOM IN ON THE DONORS

Now go back and zoom in on just the donors. Make a separate, more detailed chart specially designed for them. You may want to break down your donor categories even further for this. List them in rows down the left-hand column by whatever names or categories you have established. Start at the bottom row with donors who give less than $100, next $100-$249, then $250-$499, and then $500-$999. Above those categories, you should make special rows for the donors in your Multiple-Year Giving Society at each of the levels you offer there, even if you have not started one yet.

SAMPLE DONOR RECOGNITION/CULTIVATION PLAN

Legend: ☺ In Person · ☎ Phone · 📠 Fax · ✉ Mail · 💻 Online

Giving Level	Within 3 Days	Within 1 Week	2 Weeks Later	One Month Later	3 Months Later	6 Months Later	9 Months Later	One Year Later
Sponsor a Classroom ($25,000/yr x 5 years)	Personal Thank You/ Interview Calls from E.D.	Personal Thank You Call from Board Chair and Invite to Next Giving Society Event	Thank You Card from Classroom Signed & Personally Delivered by Kids (With Pictures)	1 on 1 Lunch with E.D. and Board Chair	Special Classroom Sponsor Event: Outline the Next Vision and Follow-Up	1 on 1 Call/ Interview from E.D.: Next Steps?	Asked to Host Small Lunch or Dinner Point of Entry for Friends; then Follow-Up	Asked to Consider Challenge Gift
Sponsor Ten Students ($10,000/yr x 5 years)		Written Thank You Letter Signed by Board Chair	Thank You Card from Student with Artwork	Classroom Tour and Lunch; Follow-Up Calls	Free Feel-Good Cultivation Event and Follow-Up	Interview and Invite to Next Free Feel-Good Cultivation Event; Assign to Donor Services Representative	Asked to Host Special Point of Entry for Friends; then Follow-Up	Call with Pledge Reminder; Asked to Consider Challenge Gift
Sponsor a Student ($1,000/yr x 5 years)	Personal Thank You/ Interview Calls from D.D. [Selected by E.D.]; Invite to Next Free Feel-Good Cultivation Event & Next Public Point of Entry	Follow-Up from D.D.: "What Else do you Need?"	Call from Donor Services Rep	Implement →			Asked to Attend Point of Entry and Invite Others	Asked to Increase Pledge at Annual Free One-Hour Ask Event
$500-$999						2nd Follow-Up Call from D.D.; Additional Solicitation: Ask to Increase Giving Level		Personal Solicitation Call or Visit from Board Member or Donor Services Representative
$250-$499						Interview and Invite to Next Free Feel-Good Cultivation Event; Assign to Donor Services Representative; Additional Solicitation: Ask to Increase Giving Level		
$100-$249		Personal Thank You from D.D.			Additional Solicitation: Ask to Increase Giving Level			Additional Solicitation and Asked to Increase Gift at Free Event
<$100		Thank You Card with Personal Note from Student or Teacher						

Spanning bands:
- Asked to be Table Captain Next Year (Within 3 Days → Within 1 Week)
- Formal IRS Thank You Letter (Within 1 Week → 2 Weeks Later)
- Free Feel-Good Cultivation Event #1 and Follow-Up (One Month → 3 Months Later)
- Asked to be Table Captains (6 Months → 9 Months Later)
- Free Feel-Good Cultivation Event #2 and Follow-Up (9 Months → One Year Later)

Next, across the top of the paper or white board, instead of writing the months of the year, you will be determining your own time categories. Each one will relate to the number of days since that donor's last gift. In other words, if your first column is labeled "within three days," you would fill in the box for each level of donor, stating what type of contact they will receive from your organization within three days of making their gift. I recommend that for any gift of $100 or more, you write in, "Personal thank-you call from development staff or board member."

Now, moving across the top row, think about how frequently that donor would need to hear from you in order to stay connected. How many contacts would you want them to have before they are asked to give again? Here are some suggested categories to write across the top:

- Within three days after the gift is received
- Within one week
- Two weeks later
- One month later
- Three months later
- Six months later
- Nine months later
- One year later

These will be the trigger points for your regularly-scheduled contacts with each donor. Of course, these do not preclude additional contact. Let's say, for example, that in the "one month later" box, you always do a personal telephone interview, or perhaps you send out a written note if you can't reach the person after three attempts. If, in the personal interview, your donors tell you about another way they would like to become involved or request special information about one of your programs, you will need more frequent and timely contact to respond to those requests.

Put yourself in your donors' shoes as you fill in each box in this chart. What kind of contact would they like six months later? Vary your media. Switch from phone to mail to online with some donors. If the donor has told you they prefer less frequent contact, how much less frequent?

At what point will you want to invite them to a Free Feel-Good Cultivation Event? How soon after that will they receive a Follow-Up Call? What other forms of personal recognition will you add? An invitation to lunch with a board member and the executive director? A special invitation to a dinner at a board member's home? You get the idea. The more customized you can make your chart, the better.

If you want to get elaborate, you can do this as a branching chart, the kind the computer folks use. If A, then B. If not A, then C, and so on.

The point is, paradoxically, to get you thinking systematically about your customized donor recognition/cultivation system. While no two donors may ever follow precisely the same path, there is a certain generic checklist with trigger points along the way that you will want to use as a template.

Just as you did with your first chart, you will want to identify who is accountable for making sure each of these contacts happens. If you have designated fund development staff or a Donor Service Representative, ultimately that will be the person. Yet you will also want to include many others in the process—board members, key volunteers, program staff, family members, etc.

The easiest way to avoid becoming overwhelmed with the complexities of the process is to simply list out the time categories suggested above (three months later, six months later, etc.) and fill in the boxes for your typical donor. Then you can customize from there.

REGULAR REVIEW

For your recognition and cultivation systems, be sure to designate someone who is accountable for bringing the team back together at least once a year, and more frequently for the donor-only chart. This will be an opportunity for everyone to assess how the system is working and further refine the process.

CHAPTER 20

KEEPING THE ASK EVENT FRESH

Once you complete your first Ask Event, including all of the post-event follow-up and data entry, it is time to celebrate with your team and then—finally—take a well-deserved break! Give yourself about a month off to reflect and recover. You have just accomplished a milestone in the life of your organization.

Make sure you get a good break from thinking about the event, because after that month is over, it is time to dive back in. The ideal Ask Event takes a full year of preparation, not just a few months.

This is the time to regroup with your team to do a deeper post-event analysis, including an honest assessment of how your organization is doing in implementing the entire Raising More Money Model, not just the Ask Event.

What were some of your larger successes that have come from putting on your Point of Entry Events, talking to people in Follow-Up Calls, and in the cultivation process? This all needs to be considered in debriefing your Ask Event. No doubt, you have won over some of the skeptics. Perhaps they are willing to jump in now as Table Captains. You may have uncovered one or more contenders to be sponsors or Challenge Gift donors for next year's event.

The second time around is a lot easier, as long as you get an early start and do all the preparation work. You now know the ropes; you have conquered the fear of the unknown. You can focus on refining and improving upon your first event, not starting from scratch. How can you ensure the excitement and energy of a full room, bustling with full tables, and an even bigger bottom-line the next time?

FOLLOW THE ENTIRE MODEL

This is often the point where groups realize that the process of putting on the Ask Event, including the results, has begun to change the way the entire organization does its fundraising. Moreover, many groups tell us at this point, that they can also see how the model affects their marketing, their volunteer and board recruitment, and even the way the program staff feel about their jobs.

This is the perfect time to solidify everyone's buy-in to the overall Raising More Money system and renew their commitment to employ a more mission-focused fundraising process going forward. This is the time to ask your board for a five-year commitment to following the model. If you are serious about developing a self-sustaining funding base, now is the time to shore up your support and invest in growing your program. This is the point at which many organizations reassemble their implementation team for the next year, adding one or more staff members to focus solely on implementing the model.

These groups recognize that the personalized cultivation process will pay off in funds raised and other support. They see that the Multiple-Year Giving Society could expand each year, leading to more significant major donors. They realize this has all been worth the risk and they are ready to wisely invest some of their hard-earned resources into growing the program.

Groups often ask us if people will tire of the event. They wonder why prior donors would want to come back to another Ask Event the next year. Ultimately, they are concerned that there is a limit to such a good thing.

However, like your organization's mission, the Raising More Money Model is built to last. Many groups have been following the model for many years. The school where the model was developed recently held its eleventh annual Sponsor-a-Student Breakfast, once again with outstanding results.

There are many ways to spruce up your event each year, while being true to the model and to your mission. The single most crucial factor for increasing your results year after year and keeping your audience fresh and enthusiastic is the passion of your Table Captains.

INCREASING TABLE CAPTAIN PASSION

You have seen by now that the secret to having a robust, successful Ask Event is the quality and number of Table Captains. It is well worth planning your Table Captain strategy a year in advance.

Remember that passion for the mission of the organization is the main prerequisite for being a good Table Captain. Many groups overlook this and default to people who are easy to recruit out of their obligation or familiarity with the organization—people whose passion may have waned a bit over time.

Take the time to make a new Treasure Map, following closely the instructions included in the Appendix, page 215. If you follow all the steps, after you have identified the many groups that your organization comes in contact with every day, you will see what resources each of these groups has in abundance. In some cases, that will be passion for your organization—precisely what you are looking for in a good Table Captain.

As you look to each group's self-interest for getting involved with your organization and consider their reasons for being connected to you, you may recall a volunteer who is also the mother of a child who was affected by the problems or issues your organization is seeking to eradicate. Now this is a woman with a personal connection to the mission. Regardless of the amount of money or the number or "quality" of contacts she has in the community, this woman would make an excellent Table Captain because she has true passion for the work of the organization.

If she were to become a Table Captain, the people she would invite to attend the Ask Event would likely say yes and attend because they know how much your work means to her. Ideally, this woman would have invited several of her friends to Point of Entry Events prior to the Ask Event. These friends would also have seen the work of the organization firsthand and, in the Follow-Up Call from a staff member or volunteer, would have had an opportunity to choose to become more involved. Therefore, several of the people at this woman's table at the Ask Event would be familiar enough with the mission of the organization that their gift would not be made strictly because of a sense of guilt and obligation to their friend the Table Captain, but because they actually believe in your work.

If you begin to use passion as your main criterion for selecting Table Captains, you will have happier Table Captains *and* better financial results.

PASSION RETREAD

Now let's revisit those dear friends of the organization who served as Table Captains merely because you asked them. While they may have had two or three empty seats at their table, they did the job, like good soldiers. Perhaps their passion for the organization was not naturally transmitted to their guests, yet once they got to the event, the passion was rekindled.

An effective strategy for increasing Table Captain passion—and therefore Ask Event size and results—is to focus on "passion retread" for these trusted insiders. If you have ever been a long-term board member or volunteer with an organization, you will know how your initial passion can wane, and being asked to fill a table at another event feels like a burden and an obligation rather than a privilege.

A method for rekindling their passion is to do this simple "passion retread" exercise at your next board or committee meeting or retreat. When people introduce themselves at the beginning of the session, have them tell their story of how they got involved or what keeps them involved with the organization. While many may say they got involved before they really understood the work being done, their reasons for staying involved now will be very moving. Often they will have a personal story or incident that instantly reconnects them.

This is also an excellent "team-building" exercise for boards or committees. I remember doing this exercise at a board retreat where one of the most outspoken members told his story briefly. The organization had saved his son's life, thanks to one of their special programs, for which this man remained a staunch advocate. Just hearing him tell his story gave everyone a deep sense of compassion for his commitment to the program. You can bet that this man made an excellent Table Captain with a full table of people who understood the value of the organization.

REVISIT THE "FIVE WAYS TO INCREASE THE BOTTOM-LINE"

Recall these five key leverage points (see Chapter 7). In addition to increasing the passion of your Table Captains, taking the time to follow these five strategies will naturally increase the size and quality of your Ask Event—and your results!

1. Get a sponsor for your event

2. Get a Challenge Gift

3. Have more Table Captains

4. Have a higher percentage of guests who are "ripened fruit"

5. Put on more Ask Events per year

ENCOURAGE REPEAT GUESTS

Most groups are surprised to find that 30-50% of their second-year Ask Event guests also attended the first year's event. It is like going back to a favorite movie or a favorite restaurant—you don't get tired of it. In fact, if anything, you are anxious to invite friends to have that same wonderful experience you had.

Repeat guests include Table Captains, donors, staff, volunteers, and board members. They return for the same reason as everyone else: because they love the organization and the event reconnects them. It is a great place to see the people associated with the organization. For many donors, this is their one time in the year when they can pay their annual pledge in-person. A surprising percentage of donors will choose to pay off the remaining four years of their pledge and some will choose to increase or extend their pledge.

Remember: this model is about building lifelong donors. For many of your first-time Multiple-Year Donors, their gift will be the first of many gifts of increasing size. This is part of the new reality of committed donors for your organization. You will need to get used to it!

CHANGING THE PROGRAM

The main concern that people have the second time around is, ironically, not with developing a stronger audience who will be more prepared to give, but with the day-of-event program.

A New Theme Each Year

As mentioned earlier, we generally recommend that your event have a theme each year. At the school where we designed the model, the Ask Event is still called the Sponsor-a-Student Breakfast, but the theme changes each year. One year we used a "back to school" theme. Another year we focused on the dreams of our students. Another year we focused on alumni stories, and yet another year on the supportive family members. One year our theme was about the teachers.

This way, though the program outline remains the same, the program content is very different each year.

For example, in the year that our theme was "supportive families," the Visionary Leader Talk was about the support of the families that is so essential to each child's success at the school. The Testimonial Speaker was a grandmother who spoke about the impact of the school on her grandson. The video included three stories of traditional and non-traditional families whose children were attending the school.

The Visionary Leader Talk is a good opportunity to link your theme to your organization's mission. This time, talk about the dream fulfilled as it would impact the family members, or the students, etc. Phrases like, "our dream is to not have to turn away any family with a child in need" can tie your vision to the theme. Rely on your mission statement for the overarching vision; people never tire of that.

So, keep the name and the program elements of your Ask Event the same each year, but let each year's theme determine the focus of the program elements.

Modifying the Pitch

Use your second Ask Event as an opportunity to honor the founding members who made their first pledge the year before. It is fine to ask them to stand up to be recognized at the event. Many groups choose to print their names on the back of the programs. That way, when it comes time for the Pitch, others in the audience will see that this is an ongoing society they might want to support. Also, the second-year Pitch can allude to some of the things the first year's funding made possible—raising teachers' salaries or offering tuition reductions.

In addition, the pitch script itself needs to recognize that there are founding members of the Multiple-Year Giving Society in the audience and thank them. We usually recommend modifying the script to say: "We invite you to join with our founding members as we grow our giving society."

Then, as your Pitch Person goes through the giving levels, be sure to call attention to the special section (which can be on the back of the pledge card) for prior donors to pay off and/or increase their pledge. At this point, the Pitch Person can say something like this: "Some of you who are here today attended this event last year and pledged your support. We thank you sincerely. We have a special section on the back of the pledge card just for you."

The back of the pledge card should contain the following options for your prior donors:

"I would like to pay my pledge in the following way:

- Add ____ more years to my previous multi-year pledge.
- Increase my financial commitment by $____ for ____ years.
- Pay off my outstanding pledge in full and increase to $____ for ____ years.
- My annual pledge payment is enclosed.
- Please contact me. I have other thoughts to share."

Units of Service

If you followed the model in designing your levels the first year, your levels should stay the same for at least ten years. If you deviated from the model and started with lower amounts or less than five year pledges, you will find yourself in an awkward dilemma. While you will see the value of changing your levels, it can be complicated to explain the change to first-year donors who thought they were giving in precisely the way you wanted them to. In this case, it is worth readjusting your levels at year two, to better position your organization for the future.

DON'T MESS WITH THE RECIPE

One major pitfall we find with subsequent Ask Events is the temptation to deviate from the formula. Changing the time of year, dollar levels of your giving units, adding in other items to the pledge card (like the mention of a capital campaign or endowment), or adding a more traditional outside speaker to the program, will each lead you astray.

Two of the other biggest mistakes groups make in subsequent Ask Events are not related to the program at all, but rather with that key leverage point: the Table Captains. First is the temptation to rely more and more on board members to be your core group of Table Captains. The fastest way for an event to stagnate and ultimately fail, over time, is to have this be just another version of strong-arming the board to invite their same group of friends to fill a table. Second is the corollary to that: the need for new Table Captains each year. This requires diligent monthly Point of Entry Events where at least 25% of the guests refer others to subsequent Point of Entry Events.

If, even for one year, you slack off on the model, you will see the results in the bottom-line of your Ask Event. The formula is so clearly spelled out and so easy to follow—you should not need to make these mistakes.

Rather, you should experience increasingly successful Ask Events each year as the model grows your base of mission-centered lifelong individual donors.

THINKING LONG-TERM: SUSTAINABLE FUNDING FOR YOUR MISSION

Congratulations on embarking on this bold, new approach, and for recognizing the longer-term impact it will have on your organization. As you no doubt have gathered by now, this is not a model or an Ask Event for people looking for a short-term fix to their cash flow problems. Implementing the Raising More Money Model requires dedication and hard work. Moreover, it requires a deep commitment to building sustainable funding for the mission of your organization from lifelong individual donors. It is about so much more than an Ask Event.

We now have many groups that have been using the model for five years or more. When they started with the model, they considered their organizations to be weak in cultivating long-term relationships with individual donors. They saw the Ask Event as a quick solution to their needs. Much to their own surprise and pleasure, by following the model, step by step, year after year, their success has evolved naturally. They now have enormously successful individual and major giving programs. Most have completed capital campaigns and are growing their endowments and planned giving programs. Rather than struggling along on the scarcity-based year-to-year treadmill, they are thriving in the new abundance-based reality of mission-centered individual giving.

Thank you for your commitment to a future of sustainable funding for your organization.

SAMPLES

*Some of the names in these sample documents
have been changed for privacy.*

Visionary Leader Talks

171

YOUNG & HEALTHY
PASADENA, CA

VISIONARY LEADER TALK

Good morning. For those of you that I have yet to meet, I am _____ and I have the honor of serving children as the Executive Director of Young & Healthy. When I was first hired at Young & Healthy, it was for a three-year pilot project, and now that three years has turned into fourteen years, and this job...has turned into a part of my soul.

I am guessing that for a lot of you, no matter how much you love your job, your possessions, even your hobbies...when push comes to shove, there is a child out there that would get top billing in your life. It might be your own child, a grandchild, niece or nephew. It might be a child you have literally rescued, or one that just makes you giggle. It might even be a child you don't know, and who will never know you. But you have—in some way—committed to them, to their well-being. You would never consider turning your back on them.

And as much as I really do love my work, I don't carry photos around of my work—but I do have them of my children. *(Pull out accordion photos.)* And I just might show them to you, whether you ask or not! Although my son Michael and my daughter Christy are slaving away at college, I am lucky to have one of my children, Stephanie, with me here today.

My children are not that different from the children that Young & Healthy serves. The parents we serve are not all that different than my husband Scott and I. They are pretty sure that *they* have the best kids. The parents we serve would love to show us pictures, and report cards, and tell how beautiful their children sound when they sing. They'd like to tell us all how cute and funny and sometimes aggravating they are. They have hopes and dreams and worries about the future for their kids.

The parents...the kids...just are not that different.

We live in the same city, but we live in really different worlds. I live in a world with lots of supports in place. I live in a world where my children certainly don't get everything they want...right Stephanie? But they certainly don't go without things they need.

I live in a world that says yes to my child when she has a little sore throat. But a world that can and *does* say *no* to another child with a seizure disorder.

I live in a world that allowed me to have my son's moles removed *before* they became melanoma, but it is also a world that says to another child who actually *has* cancer: "sorry—you'll have to wait."

It is a health care world that welcomes my daughter and all her soccer injuries, but it is a world that turns its back on another child whose parents cannot allow her to play sports for fear of an injury they cannot possibly afford.

I live in a world where my kids automatically have two, not one, dental appointments a year...more if they find a cavity. And a dentist who wasn't afraid to refer us for needed orthodontia. I live in a world where one phone call can produce a therapist who can help my children cope with an accidental death of a classmate.

But this is also a world where a child gripped with debilitating mental illness is left to their own devices.

I live in a world where I don't have to choose between glasses and groceries. I have the *luxury* of assuming that care will be available for *my three children* whenever they need it. Don't get me wrong! I am *very* grateful for the world I live in with my kids. I just hate the *other*—less fair—world.

Call me a Pollyanna. Ok, I admit, everyone calls me a Pollyanna. But I want the world to change. I know we have the power to make this a more equitable world.

We have done amazing things already here in Pasadena.

We have not yet changed the health care system, that's next week...but we have changed the community. Young & Healthy has changed this community's heart.

Now, nearly 500 volunteers all have said yes to children who live in that less-than-fair world. They have said, "Yes... you are my neighbors and I will help you." In the past fourteen years, volunteers have said "yes" to _____ *(number of)* children. These volunteers have *given away* five and a half million dollars of health care.

These are very impressive figures, and I am grateful for every gift. But as inequities continue, it *is* tough for nonprofits to raise money in this difficult economy...and we have *not* been left unscathed. Young & Healthy has tightened its collective belt. All of our programs remain intact, but we have taken fiscal steps to ensure the viability of Young & Healthy for the long haul. The wonderful staff members who make all the connections for families are now working without a pension plan, or raises. Some have voluntarily reduced their pay or their hours.

No nonprofit I know is enjoying these economic times. And yet as challenging as some of these moments are for us, we also know it is the families we serve that are hit first and hit hardest when the economy falters. Young & Healthy needs to be even more available—*not less available.* We need to stay in a position to say "yes."

Call me crazy...but I want a world where no child has to squint in the back of a classroom for lack of a $49 pair of glasses. I want a world where a child suffocated by asthma has access to a $100 nebulizer. I want a world where a family doesn't have to choose between their $500 rent and five therapy appointments. I want a world where a $5,000 surgery doesn't feel impossible.

And I hope that, beyond the mending of broken bones, broken teeth, and sometimes broken hearts...beyond providing the antibiotics, the x-rays, the physical therapy, and the taxi voucher ...I hope that we have helped children and families feel loved, cared for, and worthy of the world I get to—so luxuriously—live in.

Our lives are capable of great joy and meaning. I think it is what we are here for.

I think that there is great capacity in this room. I think we have the capacity to love and to protect our children—even those whose names we do not know, and whose faces do not appear in our wallets.

Please help us say "yes." So take good care of yourself. We need you. They need you.

NASHVILLE AREA CHAPTER
OF THE AMERICAN RED CROSS
NASHVILLE, TN

VISIONARY LEADER TALK

Good morning. This is a splendid morning in Nashville! We are gathered together here at this fine University facility. We woke up in our homes, in a warm bed. For those with families, their soft breathing may have filled the house, perhaps a dog was asleep in the hall. Or, your home may be a typically hectic affair in the morning. Bustling through bathrooms, hallways, and the breakfast table before careening out the door and spilling into traffic to get to school, to work, to the Red Cross Breakfast, and scatter across town. It is the day we expected to have. It is an ordinary day.

It is the day we planned for, the day we have taken for granted. And from here this morning, for the most part, we will have the day on our planning calendar, we will arrive at work, attend our meetings, return home this evening. Everything going as expected. Our safety and the safety of our loved ones vouched safe. Thank God for this. Yes, it is an ordinary day…the day we expected. And in that it is glorious.

My name is _____. I am Executive Director at the Nashville Area Chapter of the American Red Cross. The Red Cross taught me to be a good swimmer when I was five years old. The Red Cross taught me to be a lifeguard when I was nineteen. The Red Cross taught me to save a life using CPR and first aid when I was thirty . I have been a blood donor since 1984. I am a trained disaster relief worker. And I have worked as a staff member for the Red Cross for the past five years.

Now, many of you here this morning are familiar with the Red Cross—perhaps my brief Red Cross bio reminded you of your own history with this humanitarian organization. But some are meeting us up close for the first time.

The American Red Cross provides relief to victims of disaster and helps people prevent, prepare for, and respond to emergencies. The Red Cross is the only non-government organization that is part of federal, state, and local disaster plans. The American Red Cross manages half the nation's blood supply, and locally, all of it.

- When blood is needed, tens of thousands of volunteer donors use the Red Cross to make sure it is available without delay.

- When life-saving skills are needed, thousands of people just like you use the Red Cross to put life-savers on the streets.

- When disaster strikes, our community knows that the best trained disaster relief workers in the world will be there within two hours of being notified to help with emergency food, clothing, and shelter.

It happens from Orlinda to Antioch, Dickson to Lebanon, Green Hills to Gallatin. And, when called, our local volunteers take this desire and ability to help across America.

All Red Cross disaster assistance is provided free of charge to those who receive it, a gift of the American people to their friends, neighbors, and to you.

Being part of the Red Cross is how Nashvillians, and Americans, for that matter, have helped out in the most desperate of times.

It's about…

- Being there for your family, for your neighbor, for someone you'll never meet.

- Being there for someone when they've lost all they have.

- Being there for someone when the stakes are life or death.

The Red Cross is here because as surely as this day is gloriously ordinary, something unexpected will occur. And when it does, an ordinary day will seem like a fantasy. Jim Stevens knows this all too well. Jim is a young man, from out of town, off on his own. Two years ago, he was well along, starting his own business. Everything he owned was tied up in his new business, which he ran out of his Antioch apartment. He was building his future. Every day of Jim's life was dedicated to making this venture a success. Every day he was out beating the pavement, knocking on doors, building his dream—the American Dream.

I know this story because I was standing outside his apartment building one day a couple of winters ago, when he returned home to find over a half-dozen fire engines dousing the blaze that had already consumed twenty-three apartment units, including his. Jim was clearly in shock. I was wearing a vest that identified me as part of the Red Cross. I walked over to him, told him who I was, and asked what he needed. He didn't say much. We sat on the curb side-by-side while he wept over his shocking and devastating loss, reeling as his labors literally went up in smoke. I put my arm around him, in a feeble attempt to help him feel better. "Where do you keep your inventory?" I asked. "In there," he replied, "with all my contacts."

After a while, I walked him to a Red Cross disaster volunteer, who began getting him immediate emergency help. We couldn't replace his inventory or his contacts or his lost orders, but I knew our Red Cross would find him shelter, food, clothing, assist him with rent, and replace some other essential items right away. I knew our Red Cross would give him a good start at a most critical time. I knew he would have the best friend in town for emotional support and help recovering from this disaster. On that same day in Antioch, this type of scenario was repeated over twenty times. All disasters are big, when they happen to you.

Yes, it was an ordinary day, until something unexpected happened.

Yesterday, a disaster was usually a home fire, tornado, flood, ice storm, or industrial accident.

But since September 11, weapons of mass destruction and bio-terrorism are talked about around kitchen tables in neighborhoods and by leadership at our nation's highest levels.

Local and state officials are making plans to increase our security against these threats. And I want to tell you this morning that your Red Cross is planning for this kind of unexpected event, as well.

There are no guarantees for safety and survival during and following a disaster. But good preparation can limit damage and loss while increasing a community's overall ability to respond to and recover from a disaster. And lives will be saved.

That is why the Nashville Area Red Cross is launching *Together We Prepare* this January. *Together We Prepare*, through presentations, television, internet, print media community training, and neighborhood organizing, will dramatically increase the number of households, school, and businesses that will be ready when a good day goes bad.

- We need to make sure all of our homes and businesses have disaster plans and disaster kits. And, certainly, that 100% of all our schools do.

- We need to train 100,000 people over the next three years in first aid, CPR, and the use of an Automated External Defibrillator.

- We need to train 600 individuals to be Red Cross disaster relief volunteers, ready to respond at a moment's notice.

- We need to increase our blood supply from less than three days to at least seven days.

In 1998, when the tornadoes struck, the Red Cross system worked extremely well and trained volunteers and help from across the country came to Nashville, fed thousands, counseled hundreds, and met the immediate emergency humanitarian needs caused by that disaster.

Today, several scenarios present themselves as affecting Red Cross disaster relief in the Nashville area. In one scenario, the Nashville area cannot depend upon outside disaster relief help because transportation systems could be affected or cities quarantined.

In another scenario, significant numbers of trained volunteers may be called out of town, leaving local response short.

We are striving for Nashville to be self-sufficient when it comes to meeting humanitarian needs after a large disaster strikes. We are striving to prepare our community to limit the effects of disasters of the "ordinary" and "extraordinary" kind. And I believe that because we here in Middle Tennessee begin to prepare for a large, until recently, unthinkable disaster, lives will be saved every day when life-threatening accidents occur.

The things I am saying to you this morning, I would have told you on September 10, 2001—and you would have regarded them with an acknowledgement that these are nice things to do, but not urgent. Since September 11, no community can second-guess what might happen.

Together We Prepare is how our families can prepare for the unexpected. *Together We Prepare* is how we can be more certain that each of us will always be near someone who can save a life. *Together We Prepare* is how our community will respond to its own needs, because, I believe, there's never been a better time to help save a life. Thank you for being here today, on this ordinary of days...and thank you for being a partner in our vision to keep Nashville safe. Thank you!

SOUTHWEST AUTISM RESEARCH & RESOURCE CENTER
PHOENIX, AZ

VISIONARY LEADER TALK

Living with autism truly means living with the unexpected …like when it's 7:30 a.m. and smoke is emanating from both the microwave and toaster oven; a fountain of Gatorade is cascading from the countertop, seeping into the kitchen drawers and onto the floor; our son has just emerged from his room after meticulously laboring over tying his shoes and his long pants are on backward; and I thought we were ready to drive to school.

These are the times when I have to remind myself that learning to prepare meals and get ready independently are important abilities, as are the many other skills we've been working hard to teach our twelve-and-a-half-year-old son Matthew, who was diagnosed with autism just over a decade ago.

Living with autism means continuous learning, not just for Matthew, but for my husband Rob, our daughter Ally, and me. As a family, we seem to acquire an incredible peripheral vision, acute sense of hearing, and acceptance that the day will not often go as planned. Ironically, parents like us also start showing some dependencies of autism as our sensory systems become overloaded—overwhelmed with too much information, too many questions, too few answers, and so little control.

At SARRC, living with autism also means at least two newly diagnosed families will predictably call the Center by the end of today. And for those families, their lives have just been changed…forever.

Our hope and plan is to support them throughout their journey, along with the thousands of other affected children and family members we serve each year. With new statistics just released from the Centers for Disease Control and Prevention reporting that one in 166 children is being diagnosed with autism today, the demand for our services has never been greater and the prospects for our future, never more promising.

Since SARRC was founded in 1997, it has quickly transitioned from a small, closely held nonprofit into a mature, professional organization that is gaining local, national, and even international attention and recognition. SARRC's initial years have repeatedly demonstrated our focus, strengths, entrepreneurial spirit, and sound business principles mandated by our active and tireless board of directors to whom we are eternally grateful.

While the growth has been rapid, to keep up with the ever-increasing numbers, SARRC has expanded responsibly. We have piloted new programs to ensure their efficacy before launching major initiatives. We have strategically balanced both our research and outreach endeavors. And we have developed our financial and operational infrastructure early on to support this significant growth.

2003 was a banner year for SARRC on many fronts. You already heard about our research and groundbreaking genomics study with TGen, which represents the largest and most comprehensive genetic and molecular study ever conducted on children with autism. In addition to these efforts, SARRC advanced the development of nine new outreach programs. We launched PreStart, a new early intervention program, and HabStart, a new training program for professional therapists and paraprofessionals.

We also launched FRIENDS, a sensitivity training program that facilitates typical peer interaction in schools, which will better support this generation of children to be more accepting of and less intimidated by the growing segment of our population who live with disabilities.

Additionally, just two weeks ago, we received funding from the Nina Mason Pulliam Charitable Trust to launch a new program we call Project Gateway. This program will extend our service hours and provide special accommodations for the one in four families who have difficulties accessing SARRC's services because they are single-parent families or live in low-income households and often don't have efficient means of transportation or flexibility in their weekday schedules.

We also are very proud of our Hispanic Outreach initiative, which helped enroll and graduate nearly 100 children from Spanish-speaking families through our JumpStart early intervention last year. Many of our materials have been adapted and produced in Spanish and we applaud our entire team for this effort, especially our four Spanish-speaking staff members.

2003 also produced some fun! More than 350 family members, therapists, and volunteers were part of our family summer camp program at Whispering Hope Ranch, just outside of Payson. Here, children enjoy all kinds of therapeutic interventions, especially the animal-assisted activities. Parents learn a few coping skills and relaxation techniques. And siblings bond and partake in typical camp activities without embarrassment over the behaviors of their affected brothers and sisters. Many of TGen's scientists and staff volunteered, as they wanted to better understand our children and families beyond their DNA, RNA, and proteins.

For those of you who have not yet toured our Center, I invite and encourage you to do so. And for those of you who have been there, you can attest to our being stretched to the limit …A former lobby now serves as a parent meeting and training center; a medical exam room is now a rotating private office; our kitchen, a conference room; and a closet, our videotaping center…Depending on the time of day and day of the week, every square foot has about two to three uses! The demand for our programs and services, and the fact that we simply were running out of space, prompted SARRC two years ago to initiate a search for a much larger facility, which was critical to fulfilling our mission. I am proud to share that we have located and secured an 18,000-square-foot building that will serve as what we are proudly calling our Campus for Exceptional Children.

This new facility, which is nearly four times our current size, will significantly enhance our research capabilities and position us well to aggressively pursue programs that support affected families and children throughout their lifetimes. Plans are underway to develop this new campus, located next to St. Luke's Medical Center, where families and the community will find a state-of-the-art clinical center for research that advances major medial, social, and academic concerns. We will demonstrate best practices in therapy and early intervention, and continue expanding our parent empowerment and training programs that enable moms and dads to make informed decisions, manage home-based therapy programs, and keep their families intact. Further, we will provide vital educational resources and model laboratory classrooms that train teachers, school district personnel, therapists, and para-professionals. Pre-vocational and vocational training programs also are being developed, along with a life-skills academy that promotes independence for young adults living with autism.

With 90% of individuals diagnosed with an autistic disorder in the U.S. now under the age of twenty-one, we urgently need to design programs that will help maximize their independence, engage them in productive daily living, and ensure that they are afforded what all parents want for their children— to be healthy, secure, happy, and feel good about themselves.

Through SARRC's Campus, our goals are to better serve children with autism and their families, and to create a national model by supporting replication of appropriate elements of the campus in communities throughout Arizona and across the country. As a native Arizonan, I'm proud that soon our nation will point to Arizona as a state that's doing something great for families and our most vulnerable populations, our special children like Willy, Culley, and Jake.

This campus is for children and young adults like Molly, who at age twenty-two, is just completing her final year of high school and is without a program to attend this summer. For twenty-year-old Louis and eighteen-year-old Monique, whose sensory systems are so easily overwhelmed that today's sheltered workshops with their high ceilings and wide-open spaces are not an option. It's also for Camilla, Sean, and Garrett.

By continuing to build alliances with respected collaborators locally, nationally, and abroad, SARRC will advance its research into the causes of autism, effectively respond to the needs of families, and facilitate systemic changes in our community from health care and service delivery systems to classroom instruction, vocational skill development, and long-term care.

Our plan will only be possible if we convince each of you to join each of us. Design and construction plans are being advanced through the generous support of some of our Valley's leading development, architectural, and construction firms whose names are on the screens and featured in our most recent newsletter. We need your talents, time, services, ideas, resources, expertise, and, most of all, your tireless support. I promise you the journey will be an unexpected and memorable one, as we build our legacy together.

Gratefully, our journey at SARRC is supported by an amazing and very talented, patient, dedicated, and understanding staff. Our journey at home is supported by Matthew and Ally's loving grandparents, my sister Debbie and her family, and my extended family and family of friends who also have learned to understand the words unspoken, which are not only Matthew's, but often my own...

This was not the path I chose, nor would it be for any family. However, I have grown in many ways, perhaps differently than if things had been more predictable. What has comforted me most is the knowledge of how many people, like you, are willing to learn about autism and accept the growing number of people living with the disorder. What's inspiring to me and gives me hope is TGen and the legions of scientists, medical specialists, therapists, and volunteers committed to making a difference and advancing discoveries that ultimately will lead to a cure.

One week ago today, Matthew and I were shopping at Trader Joe's. As he repeatedly attempted to rummage through my purse looking for gum and mints or perhaps one of his videos, he was continuously mumbling the same words and phrases that were difficult for even me to discern. He then became obsessed over folding and unfolding the yellow caution stand near the check-out line and I couldn't help but notice a very curious and amused look on the cashier's face. Another clerk soon came over and assisted with bagging our groceries, which was a big relief because I just wanted to get home. I smiled politely at the two young men, took a deep breath and started to calmly explain, as I often do, that Matthew is a very special kid…But this time I was interrupted by the second clerk who exclaimed, "I know Matthew. I worked with him in Mrs. Platner's class eight years ago when I was a sixth grader at Pueblo Elementary School and it was one of the best and most memorable experiences of my life."

Life is full of unexpected moments, and your unexpected generosity will help SARRC unlock the mysteries of autism and better serve our special children and their families now and in the future. Many thanks to all of you and to our friends and family who are with us always!

Testimonials

HOSPICE SAN ANTONIO
SAN ANTONIO, TX

TESTIMONIAL

I came to know about Hospice San Antonio on November 4th of 2002, when my daughter Sandra was to be sent home from the hospital. Her doctor asked to speak with me and my grandson and told us there was nothing more that could be done—my beautiful thirty-six-year-old daughter was in the last stages of life and she as well as I wanted her to come home. When Sandra's doctor asked the social worker to speak with me about Hospice San Antonio, the social worker stated that she didn't think Hospice San Antonio came out to the city where we are from. The doctor was adamant that he wanted Hospice San Antonio to take care of Sandra. I now understand why the doctor said what he did.

A couple of hours later, a representative from Hospice came to see me and took the initial information and gave me information on Hospice San Antonio. I have to tell you, unless you have been in this situation, nothing but nothing can prepare you for this type of conversation. The Hospice nurse was very kind and sympathetic—she answered all my questions and then gave me a card. She said "think about this and call me if you are not ready to make this decision." I told her no, that this is what we had already talked about, and we were ready to go home. She gave me "the card" and said, "when you get her home, the first thing you do is call this number, no matter what time it is. We will do the rest."

On November 5th, the hospital made the arrangements with the ambulance company and Sandra was discharged. They gave me nothing but a reminder to call Hospice San Antonio. By the time we got home, a hospital bed, oxygen machine, wheelchair, and bedside potty had already arrived and been set up. I got her settled and made the phone call. About one hour after we got home, the phone rang—it was the intake nurse making sure she had the right directions. When she arrived, she spoke with Sandra, her son, my mother, her sister, and me. She examined Sandra, provided me with additional information, and made a phone call to the doctor. The doctor gave the order for Sandra's medications, and at that point I mentioned that we didn't have a twenty-four-hour pharmacy in the area and I'd have to wait until in the morning to fill her prescriptions. The nurse informed me, "Oh no, we take care of all this!" You cannot believe how surprised I was when two hours later the phone rang and it was the delivery person asking for final directions to my daughter's house. The medications arrived and I was told "if there is anything else," just call.

Anna, the assigned nurse, and her assistant arrived the next day, we set up the schedules, and again we were told "if you have any questions, just call." Over the next few days when Anna arrived, she checked medication levels and if Sandra was low on something or she needed something else, again the delivery person would arrive within a two hour period. Sandra was also assigned a volunteer who called twice a week. They would talk on the phone and she would be asked if she wanted company. The social worker called, came out to meet with us, and gave us additional information we might want to consider. The chaplain called and wanted to know if there was something he could do for us. I had no idea all this support was provided to all patients.

On Thanksgiving Day, Sandra woke and told me she no longer was going to take all of her medications, all she would take was the pain medication. I called the twenty-four-hour number, explained the situation and was told I would be receiving a phone call in a few minutes. Well, just as I was told, no more than five minutes had passed when the nurse called me, I explained the situation, and I was told what to do. At that point, my precious Sandra determined she was really on her journey home.

During the next few days, her decline was more and more evident, but the nurse and nurse's assistant never faltered. On December 7th, Anna came in to prepare us for what was to come. I told her that I wanted to wash Sandra's hair, and she offered to provide an assistant to help. I said that I could do it, and she replied "let me do this." The call was placed and I was told the assistant would be there in about an hour. The nurse left and I was told to call her if anything changed. Just as the nurse's assistant arrived, Sandra passed away. I called Anna and she said was on her way. They gave us all the time we needed with Sandra before asking me what I wanted to do. I told them that Sandra would not leave the house without taking a bath and washing her hair, so that's what we did. Anna stayed with us until after the funeral home came and left, checked out the entire family to ensure we were alright, and then left. About three hours later, she called me to make sure we were OK. Over the next few days, the chaplain called and so did the social worker, just checking to see if there was anything they could help with. You can not imagine what comfort we derived from these people—they truly care for my entire family. I was overwhelmed with their outpouring of care and support.

Bereavement counseling is also essential to help you through the rough spots and there are many. Maria is wonderful. She's allowed me to be me, and then asked me to consider her suggestions. It has made my journey a little more manageable.

I cannot believe that not all hospices are the same, but I know they are not, because when I speak with my neighbors about Hospice San Antonio, I get the same response. "We didn't get that kind of service from the hospice taking care of my husband." Not in a million years would I wish anyone go through the experience I have gone through, but if you have to, then make sure your doctors know about this wonderful organization.

I believe in Hospice San Antonio—there is none better.

ST. LOUIS CITY CASA
ST. LOUIS, MO

TESTIMONIAL

Good morning. In my professional life, I was a civil engineer, but now I'm a stay-at-home mother of three, a school and community volunteer, and a City CASA Guardian ad litem. After attending my first City CASA training session almost three years ago, I was excited to know I was among kindred spirits… people who want to make a real difference in children's lives.

In the past two and a half years, I've had three cases and have represented ten children ranging in age from three months to eighteen years. I have many stories about helping these children find safe, permanent homes, but today I want to tell you about just *one* child who is very special to me.

Mandy was seven years old and one of ten children removed from a home because of physical abuse and neglect. I became the GAL for her and her four younger siblings. At first, Mandy was a difficult child to get close to—very hyper and silly. As I learned more, though, I realized that Mandy had shouldered a lot of responsibility for such a young child—caring for her younger siblings as well as her immature twenty-one-year-old mother. She'd been sexually abused at the age of five and lived in fear of the next beating at the hands of the family she lived with.

During the next twenty-one months I became the only constant in Mandy's life and we've shared some difficult and sad times. I advocated for her when her foster placement became unsafe—when her foster mom was put under pressure for inappropriate parenting, she told Mandy it was her fault, she was too much trouble—and dropped her and her sister off on the Division of Family Services doorstep with a bag of dirty clothes, into the care of a new caseworker they'd never even met. I was there to support Mandy and reassure her she'd done nothing wrong. I was there to share her story with her new foster family and a succession of teachers, which gave them insights to addressing her problems in a caring and thoughtful way. I was there, by Mandy's side, to comfort her at the funeral of her baby sister.

We've shared a lot, Mandy and I, and I'm not sure who's benefited more. She's taught me what it means to be a survivor. I'm amazed that she's always maintained a sense of optimism in the face of such adversity. Mandy's inner strength inspires me.

Three weeks ago I was thrilled to attend the adoption of a happy and more confident Mandy into a family where she is actually the youngest child!

Weeks before, I had spoken with her about the adoption and had explained to her that this would be her *forever* home, with her *forever* mom and her *forever* sister. She calmly took my hand…looked up at me…and simply said, "Thank you."

I'm also proud to report that *all* of Mandy's siblings have been adopted in the last two months and have equally bright futures ahead of them.

My work as a City CASA Guardian isn't always easy. Sometimes getting a child to where you *know* they need to be is daunting when the system seems to put so many road blocks in your way. But I know it's one of the most important things I've ever done—or ever will do—in my life. These children inspire me every day to go outside my comfort zone to make sure they get what they need. My family lives in a safe, loving home—very different from the homes my City CASA kids come from. But my birth children are learning that the responsibility of caring for and protecting those who can't protect themselves belongs to *all of us.*

During one of our visits Mandy heard the term Guardian-ad-litem and turned that into the kid's version—*Guardian Angel,* so when she knew I was coming to visit, she always told her family and friends that her Guardian Angel was coming. I can't describe how that made me feel. It sums up for me what being a City CASA volunteer is all about. I'm only one person—but for Donald, Ashley, LaToya, Tamika, Mandy, Jerome, Tasha, Lamar, Ann, and Derek—I *was* a Guardian Angel. In fact, now I truly believe that *every single child* deserves their own Guardian Angel.

SOLV
HILLSBORO, OR

TESTIMONIAL

Good Morning, my name is _____ and I am a senior at West Linn High School. I have been lucky enough to have been exposed to this wonderful organization called SOLV through a program at my school called Green Team. Green Team consists of learning about watershed restoration techniques, applying those skills, and watching the change.

Green Team has also taught me about the pressing issues that are affecting my local watershed, such as housing developments destroying stream flow or impervious surfaces heating up the water entering our streams and rivers.

Living in Oregon has always given me great pride, whether it was hiking at Oneonta Falls on a beautiful summer day, or watching people build sand castles in the rain at Cannon Beach. I have always been proud to be an Oregonian, which is why I am committed to taking actions today to ensure our state is as beautiful in fifty years as it is today.

I have been a member of Green Team for two years now. Our main site has been in West Linn, at Wilson Creek. It has been really satisfying to be able to see what kind of progress we have made. Where there were once six-foot-tall blackberry bushes, there is now a healthy diverse native plant community. It was so exciting to finally see deer tracks next to the creek the fall after our planting in the spring.

Through the amazing leadership and dedication of our Green Team leaders, our partnership with SOLV and my Environmental Science teacher Mr. _____, I have learned that the change has to start now if we want a beautiful Oregon tomorrow.

My peers and I keep hearing that we are the future, that we need to be the change, and we are now starting that change, but we need support. A single string floating in the water makes little difference, but many strings woven together can form a net and clean up a river. We want all generations to band together and take a step forward as one. As Mr. _____ says, "If not us, then who, and if not now, then when?"

Pitch Scripts

MICHIGAN MOTHERS AGAINST DRUNK DRIVING
LANSING, MI

PITCH SCRIPT

Thanks to Melanie and Chris for sharing their stories with us of how MADD has touched their lives.

Hi, I'm _____, and I'd like to add my welcome and thanks to all of you for being here with us today. I'm fortunate to have been involved with Michigan Mothers Against Drunk Driving for several years. Through my role as a prosecutor, I have witnessed the devastation that drunk driving brings to the lives of individuals and families. I have also witnessed the efforts of MADD as it combats the problems of impaired driving. MADD has made and continues to make a difference. It does so in the lives of victims and for every one of us here as it helps to create a safer community.

Since its founding in 1980, MADD has helped save nearly 270,000 lives. This is the kind of result that clearly indicates MADD's ability to make us safer as we travel the roadways of our communities. As you have also just heard, MADD makes a difference in the lives of young people. The potential for ultimately accomplishing MADD's mission hinges on MADD's continued success in its work with the young, raising a new generation that will forever change the way everyone thinks about drinking and driving and underaged drinking.

When you came here today, most of you did not know exactly what we were going to ask you for in terms of your financial support. You probably came today because a friend invited you or because you already are familiar with our organization. But now that you've heard the full MADD Michigan story and met some of our wonderful people, it's my privilege to ask you to make a financial investment in our ongoing success. This is not just an investment in MADD; it truly is an investment in our own futures, and I believe that it is one of the most important investments that any of us can make.

When we looked at what we wanted to ask you for, we decided to request what we really need most—financial support for our day-to-day operations. Unfortunately, there are thousands of young people in this incredibly successful community who need the support of a program like those that MADD offers in order to reach their full potential. Your support can help ensure that we can reach these young people well into the future.

To build a stronger foundation for expanding our programs and to provide a stable future for MADD Michigan, today we are launching a brand-new partnership—a Multiple-Year Giving Society we are calling the Lighthouse Keepers Society. If you have been inspired by what you've seen today, I ask you now to consider joining me this morning as a founding member of our Society.

Now I'd like to ask the Table Captains to pass out the pledge cards. *(Pause only briefly.)*

Starting at the top of the card, the Lighthouse Keepers Society is meant to give you a sense of what your contribution can do. Your contribution will go toward the unrestricted operating funds of MADD Michigan.

1. The first giving level in the Lighthouse Keepers Society is a pledge of $1,000 each year for five years. We call this our "Lantern" level because $1,000 is approximately the cost of providing an awareness program to 1,000 students. So if you would consider a gift at this level, which is an average of just $83 per month (or think of it as a latte a day), your gift would help us to shine the light of awareness even brighter for a student like Chris.

2. The next giving level in the Lighthouse Keepers Society is $5,000 a year for five years. This is our "Fresnel" level. A fresnel lens enables spotlights to have a magnified intensity. If you would consider a gift of $5,000 each year for five years, you would allow us to magnify our message to 5,000 young

people each year for five years, helping to raise up a generation that will clearly understand that you do not drink and drive.

3. We know that many of you are part of a company or foundation, or you may just be in a position to give more. So the next level is the "Beacon," which lets you have a far-ranging impact on the lives of those who have been tragically impacted by a drunk driving crash. If you would consider a gift of $10,000 a year for five years, that would be a major boost in being able to sponsor a victim advocate and give care to individuals and families who have experienced a devastating death or injury like Melanie's family.

If you are willing to join today as a founding member of the Lighthouse Keepers Society, I give you my personal thanks for your generous support.

Although I started by introducing the Lighthouse Keepers Society, we know and respect that you may prefer to give at a different level, and so we provide the next line just for you. On this line, please tell us how much you would like to give and for how many years.

We truly appreciate whatever level of support you can provide and we ask that you make the first payment on your pledge today.

Perhaps you would like to consider a gift of stock or something else. Or, you simply have some great ideas for us. If so, please check the next box, that one that says, "Please contact me, I have other thoughts to share."

I know that many of you are still writing, but, if I could have your attention here for just a moment. It's important that you really hear what I'm about to say. Whatever gift you have chosen to make today—whether you have become a founding member of our Lighthouse Keepers Society, made a gift at a different level, or have given the gift of your valuable time to attend today, we sincerely thank each and every one of you on behalf of the wonderful people that we serve.

I'll give you some time now to finish filling out the cards; when you are finished, please pass your envelopes back to your Table Captain.

Whether or not you chose to make a pledge today, we really appreciate that you took time out of your busy lives to be here this morning to learn more about Mothers Against Drunk Driving.

Now, I'll turn the program back to _____ to wrap up.

BUFFALO AND ERIE COUNTY HISTORICAL SOCIETY
BUFFALO, NY

PITCH SCRIPT

Hello, my name is _____. My involvement with the Historical Society began with *(give brief personal history with organization).*

I am very proud to be involved with this regional treasure.

Today, you've heard our organization's story as well as the stories of several Western New Yorkers—people just like you. You've met a couple of Presidents of the United States and some of our staff, board members, and volunteers, who have already taken their places in history.

My job now is to ask for your financial investment in the ongoing work of the Buffalo and Erie County Historical Society. To ask you to take your own place in history.

We know that most of you did not know what we were going to ask of you today. You came because a friend invited you.

We are asking you for what we really need the most—support for the day-to-day care of our collections and archives and the day-to-day operation of our programs and services, including those for students and educators.

For me, the most exciting part of this program is right now—when we launch something brand-new—the History Makers Society. Our goal for the History Makers Society is to provide the Historical Society with a stable base of operating revenue for a five-year horizon. My wife Kathy and I have already made our decision to become founding members of the History Makers Society. *(Recognize any other inspirational gifts here.)* We are taking our place in history today. If you have been inspired by what you've seen today, we ask you to join us in making a multiple-year commitment by becoming a founding member of the History Makers Society.

Now, I'd like to ask the Table Captains to pass out the pledge cards. *(Pauses as they are passed out.)* Let me walk you through the card.

1. The first giving level in the History Makers Society is $1,000 a year for five years to "Collect a Story," like the stories you've heard this morning. You can help ensure that we have the resources—staff, supplies, and equipment—to collect a uniquely Western New York story for posterity. Please check off the first box on the pledge card if you can do this.

2. We know that some of you are capable of giving more. The next level allows you to "Preserve a Story" for $5,000 a year for five years. Imagine the difference that would make—our having the resources to ensure that the stories that we collect are protected and cared for with the very best and most current museum practices. If you can do this, check the second box.

3. Moving down to the next box on your card. Some of you may be part of a company or foundation, or again, you are just in a position to consider giving more. Your investment of $10,000 a year for five years will allow us to "Tell a Story"—to share the stories that we have collected and preserved so that future generations will appreciate their heritage. If you want to ensure that we have the resources to tell these stories in ways that engage city and suburban families, old and young, please check the third box.

Again, we know that most of you had no idea what we were going to ask of you today. We started out asking you to become a founding members of our brand-new History Makers Society. We are so very grateful to those of you who have chosen to do that.

Now we'd like to ask those of you who have not yet made a commitment to tell us how much you would like to give and for how many years. Please check the fourth box and fill in the blanks.

We truly appreciate whatever you can give. Please do consider a multiple-year gift. This kind of commitment provides us with the stability that we need to plan for the future.

Whatever gift you've decided to make, we ask that you make your first payment today. As you can see, we are happy to take credit cards!

Finally, perhaps you would like to have more information about us or would like to take a behind the scenes tour, or would like to discuss a special idea that's occurred to you this morning. Please check the last box, the one that says: "Please contact me. I have other thoughts to share." Believe me when I say that having the opportunity to tell you our story this morning has been as important to us as a monetary gift. We can't ask anyone to invest in something they don't understand, and you have given us the chance to begin that process of understanding.

I'll give you some time now to finish filling out the cards. Please pass your envelopes back to your Table Captain when you're done.

(Looks up, pauses until 2/3 of the pledge cards have been passed in as indicated by signals from the Table Captains.)

Thank you all for investing in the heritage of your community this morning. Truly, you have taken your place in history today. We welcome the founding members of the History Makers Society and thank you for your bold and defining commitment to protecting your heritage. To others of you who made gifts this morning, we are very grateful for your faith in us and for your pledges of support. Also, we are so thankful to all of you for choosing to share the valuable gift of your time with us. We know there are so many other things that you could have done with this time. Please accept our gratitude and our great joy in renewing our friendship with you or beginning a new friendship.

BOYS & GIRLS CLUBS OF LAS VEGAS
LAS VEGAS, NV

PITCH SCRIPT

Thank you all for sharing your stories with us. Some of you already know I am on the Foundation Board for the Boys & Girls Clubs of Las Vegas. I've been involved with this great organization for ten years because *I am passionate about this organization* and because I have seen firsthand that it *really has* made a difference to our community's kids.

As you've just heard, there are many children and many others who love the Clubs. In the last hour, I hope you've learned a bit about the services and programs offered by the Boys & Girls Clubs of Las Vegas and I hope you've seen what a vital, important role the Clubs play in our community. It is a continuing privilege for me to be part of this organization.

I want to thank all of you who are here today who already support us in so many ways. We are thrilled to have you here. We are grateful to those who came just to learn more about the Clubs and their impact. I hope we have inspired you.

When you came here today, most of you did not know what we were going to ask for in terms of your financial support. You probably came today because a trusted friend invited you or because you were already familiar with our organization. But now that you've heard the full story about Boys & Girls Clubs of Las Vegas and what we'd like to accomplish in the near future, it's *my privilege to ask you to make a financial investment* in our ongoing success. This is *not* just an investment in Boys & Girls Clubs of Las Vegas. It truly is *an investment in our own future—our children*, and I believe it is one of the most important investments *any of us* can make.

When we looked at what we wanted to ask you for, we decided to request what we really need most—financial support for our day-to-day operations. Unfortunately, there are thousands of children right here in this incredibly successful community who *need a positive, safe, and affordable place to go.* Your support can help ensure that we can reach out to many more children who need the Boys & Girls Clubs well into the future.

To build a stronger foundation for expanding our reach and to provide a stable future for the Boys & Girls Clubs of Las Vegas, today we are launching *a brand-new partnership*—the Every Kid Counts Multiple-Year Giving Club. If you have been inspired by what you've seen and heard, I ask you now to consider joining me this afternoon as a founding member of our Every Kid Counts Club.

I have a really exciting announcement, too. *(Name of challenge donor)* has generously offered us a challenge grant to help us meet our goal to serve more children. *(Name of challenge donor)* will match up to *$50,000* any funds raised today to support the operation of our clubhouses in the year 2004. This is an incredible opportunity for which we are so grateful. *(Name of challenge donor)*, will you please stand now so we can acknowledge you?

(Audience applauds.)

We are so appreciative of *(name of challenge donor)*'s generosity. This challenge grant allows us to double the size of any gift you make today. $100 turns into $200, $5,000 turns into $10,000. If your company has a matching gift program, then a gift can generate four times its original size. What a great incentive.

Now, I'd like to ask the Table Captains to pass out the pledge cards.

(Pause only briefly, then explain card very quickly.)

These pledge levels are in some ways symbolic, but they represent *the real costs* of conducting our programs.

1. The first giving level in the Every Kid Counts Multiple-Year Giving Club is a pledge of $1,000 each year for five years. $1,000 is the cost of funding one boy and one girl in a clubhouse for an entire year. So if you will consider a gift at this

level, which is an average of just $83 per month—or think of it as a latte a day—your gift will allow us to provide a safe and positive place for two children for each of the next five years.

2. If you would consider a gift of $10,000 dollars each year for five years, you will allow us to serve even more kids—the equivalent of twenty kids each year for the next five years.

3. We know some of you may be part of a company or foundation, or you may just be in a position to give more. If you would consider a gift of $25,000 a year for five years, you will support fifty kids each year. If you can give at this level, your gift will have a *major impact* in allowing us to reach out to many youth in Las Vegas who need Boys & Girls Clubs' services and programs.

We are incredibly grateful to you for making a difference in these kids' lives.

If you are joining me today as a founding member of the Every Kid Counts Club, my personal thanks for your generous support!

Although I started by introducing the Every Kid Counts Multiple-Year Giving Club, we know and respect that we all have different financial means, and so we provide the next fill-in-the-blank line just for you. On this line, please tell us how much you would like to give and for how many years. We *truly appreciate* whatever level of support you can provide.

I hope that many of you have already chosen one of these options. If not, perhaps you want more information, would like to take a tour of the Clubs, or you simply have some great ideas for us. Please check the last box, the one that says "Please contact me, I have other thoughts to share."

(Pause and SLOW down for next part.)

I know many of you are still writing but, if I could have your attention here for just a moment, I have something important I really want to share with you:

Whatever gift you have chosen to make today—whether you have become a founding member of our Every Kid Counts Club, made a gift at a different level, or if you have simply given the gift of your valuable time to be here, I sincerely thank each and every one of you. You are doing so much just by being here this afternoon to help us serve young children who really need us. Thank you.

I'll give you some time now to finish filling out the cards and when you are finished, please pass your envelopes back to your Table Captain.

(Pause just briefly to allow guests to turn in their pledge cards.)

We really appreciate you taking time out of your busy lives to be here this afternoon to learn more about Boys & Girls Clubs of Las Vegas. We hope you had a great time and increased your knowledge about this extraordinary organization. Thank you all for coming, and have a great day!

Pledge Cards

ALPHA USA PHILADELPHIA
PHILADELPHIA, PA

PLEDGE CARD

Alpha USA Philadelphia
Power to
Transform
Fundraising Breakfast

We invite you to join us in changing our community through the transforming power of the Alpha Course.

I would like to become a founding member of the Transformation Alliance and help transform:

_____ Gift of Hope: $1,000 per year for 5 years—changing 100 lives

_____ Gift of Faith: $10,000 per year for 5 years—serving 50 churches

_____ Gift of Transformation: $25,000 per year for 5 years—serving a community

I would like to contribute in other ways:

_____ Contribute $_____ for _____ years.

_____ Please contact me. I have other thoughts to share.

Payment:

_____ My check is enclosed made payable to Alpha USA/Philadelphia.

_____ Please charge my Visa/MC/Amex/Discover #_____Exp._____

_____ Please contact me about paying my pledge with stock.

_____ My company will match my gift.

_____ My gift is in memory of _____ .

We will bill you in (month) for your annual pledge, unless you request otherwise.

Date: _____

Name with title: _____

Organization/Company: _____

Address: _____

City: _____ State: _____ Zip: _____

Day Phone: _____ Evening Phone: _____

E-mail Address: _____

Alpha North America is a tax-exempt 501 (c) (3) charitable organization;
therefore donations are tax deductible consistent with IRC Section 170.

ARTHRITIS FOUNDATION, NEBRASKA CHAPTER
OMAHA, NE

PLEDGE CARD

Arthritis Foundation, Nebraska Chapter
Commitment to a Cure
Fundraising Luncheon

I would like to become a founding member of the Arthritis Alliance:

_____ Prevent: $1,000 per year for 5 years

_____ Control: $10,000 per year for 5 years

_____ Care: $25,000 per year for 5 years

I would like to contribute in other ways:

_____ Contribute $_____ for _____ years.

_____ Please contact me. I have other thoughts to share.

Payment:

_____ My check is enclosed, made payable to Arthritis Foundation, Nebraska Chapter.

_____ Please charge my Visa/MC #_____Exp._____

_____ Please contact me about paying my pledge with stock.

_____ My company will match my gift.

We will bill you in November for your annual pledge, unless you request otherwise.

Date: _____

Name: _____

Company/Residence: _____

Address: _____

City: _____ State: _____ Zip: _____

Day Phone: _____ Evening Phone: _____

E-mail Address: _____

NATIONAL ASSOCIATION OF MOTHERS' CENTERS
LEVITTOWN, NY

PLEDGE CARD

National Association of Mothers' Centers
"Motherhood & Apple Pie" Fundraising Breakfast

I would like to become a founding member of the Mothers Matter Giving Circle:

_____ Gift of Seeds: $1,000 per year for 5 years

_____ Gift of Roots: $5,000 per year for 5 years

_____ Gift of Wings: $10,000 per year for 5 years

I would like to contribute in other ways:

_____   Contribute $_____ for _____ years.

_____   Please contact me. I have other thoughts to share.

Payment:

_____   My check is enclosed, made payable to NAMC.

_____   Please charge my (circle one): Visa   Mastercard   Discover   American Express

         #_____ Exp. Date_____

         _____   _____
         (name as it appears on card)   (Signature)

_____   Please contact me about paying my pledge with stock.

_____   My company will match my gift.

You will be billed in May for your annual pledge, unless you request otherwise.

Name: _____ Date: _____

Address: _____

City: _____ State: _____ Zip: _____

Day Phone: _____ Evening Phone: _____

E-mail Address: _____

APPENDIX

CREATING A TREASURE MAP
Excerpted from "Raising More Money—The Point of Entry Handbook"

As you begin to see the merit of Point of Entry Events, you will naturally wonder who to invite to them. Given the personal nature of this model, it only makes sense to start with the people who already are connected to you in some way. You can branch out from there, following the stream of passion and natural word-of-mouth connections that link people. Before you know it, the whole system will snowball.

Rather than spending time trying to interest the obvious wealthy donors in your community who may not know or care about your organization, take the time to brainstorm about the natural supporters who are lurking right under your nose. We use the term "Treasure Map" because it identifies the natural treasure around you right now. You don't have to go out of your way to find these people. You don't have to make your selections based on wealth or social status. Include everyone and brainstorm away.

LEARNING TO DRAW A TREASURE MAP
This brainstorming exercise is best done with a team of people—ideally, the same team that will be involved in implementing the model over the next year or two. The more diverse your team members, the more diverse the Treasure Map. At some point, you will want to do this exercise with your board as well. If you are the person who will be leading the group through the process, be sure to practice it first with a small group of staff members, family, or friends.

Get out a large piece of paper and colored markers and lead your team through the process. Begin by drawing a circle in the center of the page. Put the name of your organization in the circle.

Then surround your organization, like the spokes on a wheel, with all the other groups you come in contact with on a regular basis. Start with groups like your board, staff, volunteers, donors and funders, vendors, and other groups in the community that you interact with regularly.

TREASURE MAP
GROUPS AND ORGANIZATIONS

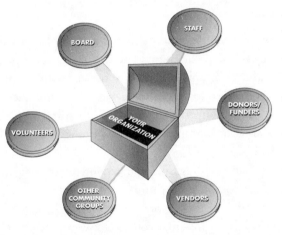

You may be able to subdivide groups like your board or staff further into former board, former board presidents, founding board members, etc. Similarly, your volunteers may be subdivided by the type of projects they are involved with. United Way, for example, has many substrata of loaned executive volunteers—depending on the industry they came from or the industry they will be soliciting. Red Cross volunteers may be subcategorized as blood volunteers, disaster volunteers, health and safety volunteers, and so on.

Take the time to brainstorm as many groups as you can think of. You can lump all the civic groups under one category. All the other community organizations you interact with may be a group or you may choose to subdivide them into categories like law enforcement, schools, other arts organizations, etc.

The more detail you can put into the Treasure Map as you list these groups, the more you will be able to target their specific resources and self-interests in the later steps of the Treasure Map process.

RESOURCES IN ABUNDANCE

Now, with a differently colored pen or marker, list the resources which each of these groups has in abundance. Why? Because this is an abundance-based model of fundraising. It presumes people will naturally want to give that which they have plenty of.

Most of us do not like saying no; it makes us feel mean and uncaring. People would rather say yes when you ask them. It is much easier for them to say yes if you are asking them to give you something you know they already have in excess. For some people you may not know what that is, but it usually doesn't take long to find out when you think about who you could ask.

Go back to the Treasure Map and start listing out the abundant resources of your board, staff, volunteers, etc. Take the time to look closely at each group or subgroup. You will notice that their resources may be different. For example, your board in general might have an abundance of passion, commitment, expertise, contacts, and money.

TREASURE MAP
ABUNDANT RESOURCES

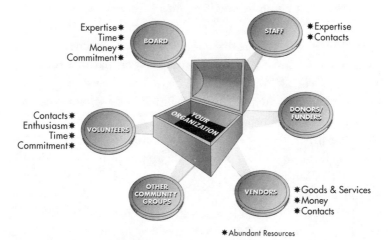

* Abundant Resources

Yet your former board presidents may have additional resources, such as a long-term commitment to your organization or certain connections in the community.

Your volunteers might have an abundance of time, expertise, connections, and money as well. When you categorize volunteers by the type of program they are involved with, you will see more resources. Literacy tutors, for example, may have an abundance of teaching skill or an abundance of contacts in the educational field or an abundance of passion and personal stories to share from the people they have tutored.

How about your staff? They have an abundance of passion, firsthand stories about the good work of your organization, time (because they are being paid for their time at work), and expertise. Staff in different programs and departments will have different stories and different connections. Hospice nurses will have had direct contact with family members. Department directors may have more contact with the doctors. Take the time to do this with each group. What resources do they have in abundance?

SELF-INTEREST

Next, go back over each group and ask what their self-interest would be in coming to your Point of Entry Event. What is the value or benefit for them in attending?

Let's pause a minute to talk about self-interest. Self-interest is a good thing. It drives everything we do. For example, you have a definite self-interest in reading this book. Maybe that self-interest is finding new ideas, maybe it is pleasing the boss, or maybe it is because you wanted a break from your work. Self-interest is always there, and as a person who is interested in raising funds, you should think of it as a very useful resource.

Self-interest can range from the most negative and selfish motives all the way to the most noble and inspiring. Consider the full range of self-interest as you go back to your Treasure Map and list the self-interests of each group.

Consider, for example, your donors or funders. What benefit does being connected to you have for them? Ask yourself, "What is

TREASURE MAP
SELF INTERESTS

Expertise ✱
Time ✱
Money ✱
Commitment ✱
Make a Difference ✪
Feel Good ✪
Personal Connection ✪
Please the Boss ✪

BOARD

STAFF

✱ Expertise
✱ Contacts
✪ *Paycheck*
✪ *Make a Difference*

Contacts ✱
Enthusiasm ✱
Time ✱
Commitment ✱
Make a Difference ✪
Contribute Talents ✪
Learn New Skills ✪
Socialize ✪

VOLUNTEERS

YOUR ORGANIZATION

DONORS/ FUNDERS

✱ Money
✱ Time
✱ Contacts
✪ *Tax Write-off*
✪ *Feel Good*
✪ *Making a Difference*

OTHER COMMUNITY GROUPS

VENDORS

✱ Goods & Services
✱ Money
✱ Contacts
✪ *Look Good to Others*
✪ *They Really Care*
✪ *New Business Contacts*

✱ Abundant Resources
✪ *Self-Interests*

in this for them?" Yes, they may want a tax write-off, but this is rarely the sole reason for making a gift. For most donors, a major self-interest is feeling good about making the gift and feeling they are making a difference. For some donors, self-interest is paying back someone for something they once received. Or maybe they have a personal connection to the services you offer. Or they feel that giving to your organization is a kind of insurance, that what you are committed to preventing won't happen to them. Guilt can be a self-interest, as well as impressing others and looking good. Maybe they are giving because they think it will help their child or grandchild to be accepted into your private school or college.

Look at the self-interest of your volunteers. Why are they involved with you? Perhaps it is to make a difference, to contribute their talents, to learn new skills, to build their resume for their next job, to give back, to feel important, to keep busy, and on and on. What about your board? For some, their self-interest is to please a boss who "asked" them to serve on your board. For others, it is a personal connection, a way of giving back, or a feel-good thing.

Donor for donor, self-interest is a key driver of your self-sustaining individual giving program. The sooner you know your donors' self-interest, whatever it may be, the easier it will be to customize your fundraising program to their needs. Down the road, as they become lifelong donors, you will want to think back to the self-interest that led to their involvement in the first place.

FANTASY GROUPS

Next, looking back at your Treasure Map, add in some fantasy categories. Who is not yet on your map that you would love to have associated with your organization? Whose involvement would leverage a whole world of support and credibility? Add those people to your Treasure Map, too. Some typical fantasy categories include celebrities, athletes, corporate executives, and media figures. For some organizations, having the support of a local opinion leader, a religious leader, or an expert on your issue could quickly leverage your story into the larger community.

TREASURE MAP
FANTASY GROUP

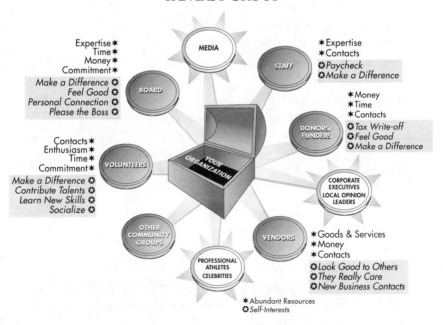

Let yourself play with this one. This is why it is fun to do a Treasure Map with a group of people.

CONNECTING THE GROUPS

Finally, draw connecting lines between those groups on your Treasure Map who already talk to each other. You will see instantly how fast news travels. If a handful of people come to your sizzling Point of Entry Event, who else will they tell?

If your staff talks to your volunteers, draw a connecting line between those two groups. If your board and vendors talk only occasionally, you might draw a dotted line. For those groups who don't talk to each other at all, draw no connecting lines. Be sure to include your fantasy groups. Who on your organization's Treasure Map already might be talking with them? It is worth taking the time to go through this one category at a time. It can spark many insights.

TREASURE MAP
WHO TALKS TO WHOM?

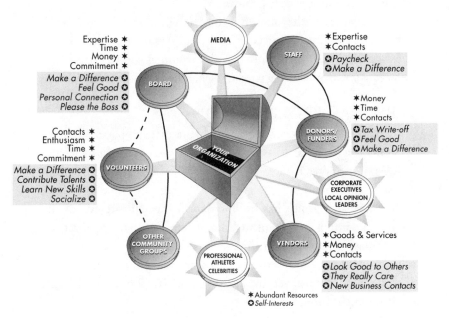

Before moving on, stand back from your Treasure Map and notice which groups have the most lines connecting them to other groups. There may be so many lines leading to or from that group that it looks like a traffic jam. What does that tell you? These groups are key to leveraging others. They could naturally invite the people in these other groups to attend your Point of Entry Events because they are speaking to them all the time anyway.

A frequent example of a traffic-jam group is your staff. The staff is likely to be one group on the Treasure Map that talks to nearly every other group. What does that tell you? It should tell you that staff buy-in to your Point of Entry system is critical to your success. You will want to make a special effort to involve staff in the process. The easiest way to do this is to have special staff-only Point of Entry Events early on in the process. The staff can be invaluable in critiquing and refining the content at your Point of Entry. I remember how much we modified what we said at our school tours after taking the teachers through the tours and debriefing them individually about how to talk about the curriculum.

Conversely, if they have not fully bought into the process, the staff can be your biggest adversary. Go out of your way to let the staff know how essential their input is and how much you will need their support as you begin having regularly scheduled Point of Entry Events.

PERSONAL TREASURE MAP

Next, give each team member a blank piece of paper and have them make a personal Treasure Map for themselves. Start by having people put their own names in the middle. Then have them go through the same steps of adding the groups they naturally come in contact with, what each group has in abundance, the self-interests of the groups in coming to a Point of Entry Event for your organization, their fantasy groups, and the lines connecting those who know each other. Give them enough time to get into doing the exercise. They probably will be surprised by all the treasure they have. Give them the time to go through all the steps.

Now, assuming your team has already attended a Point of Entry Event and knows what you are talking about, you can ask them to look back to their personal Treasure Maps and make a list of ten to twenty individuals they would feel comfortable inviting to a Point of Entry. Encourage them to have their list include people from each group on their Treasure Map, not just the "safest" groups of friends and family. Once they see the self-interest people have in coming to a Point of Entry, inviting them will become more of a game than a chore. They will realize that the person at the health club had already mentioned their interest in the environment or their mother's health problem. In other words, these people might actually want to come to learn more about your organization.

Some people on your team will have long, long lists of people they could invite. Do not make them feel awkward or embarrassed. There will naturally be people with more contacts than others. Long-time volunteers may have extensive lists of former volunteers they would like to invite. People in the health care profession may have more people on their personal Treasure Maps with self-interest in your health care work. Give everyone the time to make their lists or tell them to finish them after the meeting.

THE FORMULAS

THE FORMULAS

I. Point of Entry
   A. Attendance and Referrals
      1. You should expect a no-show rate of 30-40% at each Point of Entry Event
      2. At least 25% of your POE guests should be referring others to POE's
II. Ask Event
   A. Table Captains and Guests
      1. To determine your monetary goal:
         Number of guests at the event divided by two X $1,000 = Total you will raise including the five year pledges (Example: An Ask Event with 200 people should raise $100,000, including pledges)
      2. 100% of your Ask Event Table Captains must have attended a POE
      3. 20% of Ask Event attendees must have been to a POE ("ripened fruit")
      4. You should expect to lose 15% of your Ask Event Table Captains and 15% of their final guest list
      5. Staff should make up less than 10% of your Table Captains
   B. Gifts and Pledges
      1. To determine your Units of Service:
         a. If your single largest unrestricted gift from an individual in the past two years is **less than $10,000**, your levels will be:
            • $ 1,000 X 5 years
            • $ 5,000 X 5 years
            • $10,000 X 5 years
         b. If your single largest unrestricted gift from an individual in the past two years is **$10,000 or more**, your levels will be:
            • $ 1,000 X 5 years
            • $10,000 X 5 years
            • $25,000 X 5 years
      2. 40% of Ask Event guests will fill out the pledge sheet and turn it in on the day of the event
      3. 5-10% of Ask Event attendees will typically give at the $1,000 (for five years) level
      4. Expect 95% or better payoff rate on pledges from Multiple-Year Donors
      5. Approximately 60-70% of your Ask Event donors will be new donors
      6. Aim to have 100% of your Multiple Year Giving Society Donors attend your Ask Event in subsequent years either as Table Captains or VIP's

ABOUT THE AUTHOR

Terry Axelrod is the CEO and founder of Raising More Money, an organization that trains and coaches nonprofit organizations to implement a mission-based system for raising sustainable funding from individual donors. This system ends the suffering about fundraising and builds passionate and committed lifelong donors.

With over thirty years of experience in the nonprofit field, Axelrod has founded three nonprofits in the fields of health care and affordable housing. She realized early in her career that the only path to sustainable funding was to systematically connect donors to the mission of the organization, then involve and cultivate them until they were clearly ready to give—in short, to treat donors the way you would treat a close friend or family member, someone with whom you planned to have a lifelong relationship.

Axelrod created the Raising More Money Model in 1996 after serving as Development Consultant to Zion Preparatory Academy, an inner-city Christian Academy in Seattle, from 1992-1995. There she designed and implemented fundraising and marketing programs which yielded $7.2 million in two and a half years as well as national recognition of the program, including a cover story in the *Chronicle of Philanthropy*.

Author of two previous books, *Raising More Money—A Step-by-Step Guide to Building Lifelong Donors* and *Raising More Money— The Point of Entry Handbook*, Axelrod is also a sought-after speaker, both nationally and internationally. Her passionate commitment to the possibility of sustainable funding for all nonprofits drives the mission of Raising More Money and each of its programs. "The donors are truly out there—wanting to contribute; it's up to the organizations to connect donors powerfully to their work and nurture that connection over time. Our programs give each organization the tools to do that successfully."

Axelrod currently serves as a Director of the American Association of Fundraising Counsel, a Trustee of the Greater Seattle Chamber of Commerce, and Life Trustee of Swedish Medical Center. She received her Master's of Social Work and Bachelor's Degrees at the University of Michigan, and she resides in Seattle with her husband, Alan, and their two children.

ADDITIONAL INFORMATION
AND RESOURCES

Visit our Web site at www.raisingmoremoney.com to:

- Subscribe to our free bi-weekly electronic newsletter, the Raising More Money E-New$.

- Register for one of our many free or inexpensive introductory sessions.

- Register for the two-day Raising More Money 101 Workshop.

- Purchase books and videos or DVDs about Raising More Money.

- Learn more about the Raising More Money Next Step donortracking system.

- Browse the Raising More Money archives for additional information on building sustainable funding from lifelong individual donors.

INDEX